Collins

EXCURSIONS

A course in Social Studies

Teacher's Manual 5 Revised Edition

Authors

Meenakshi Wattal | Debahuti Das

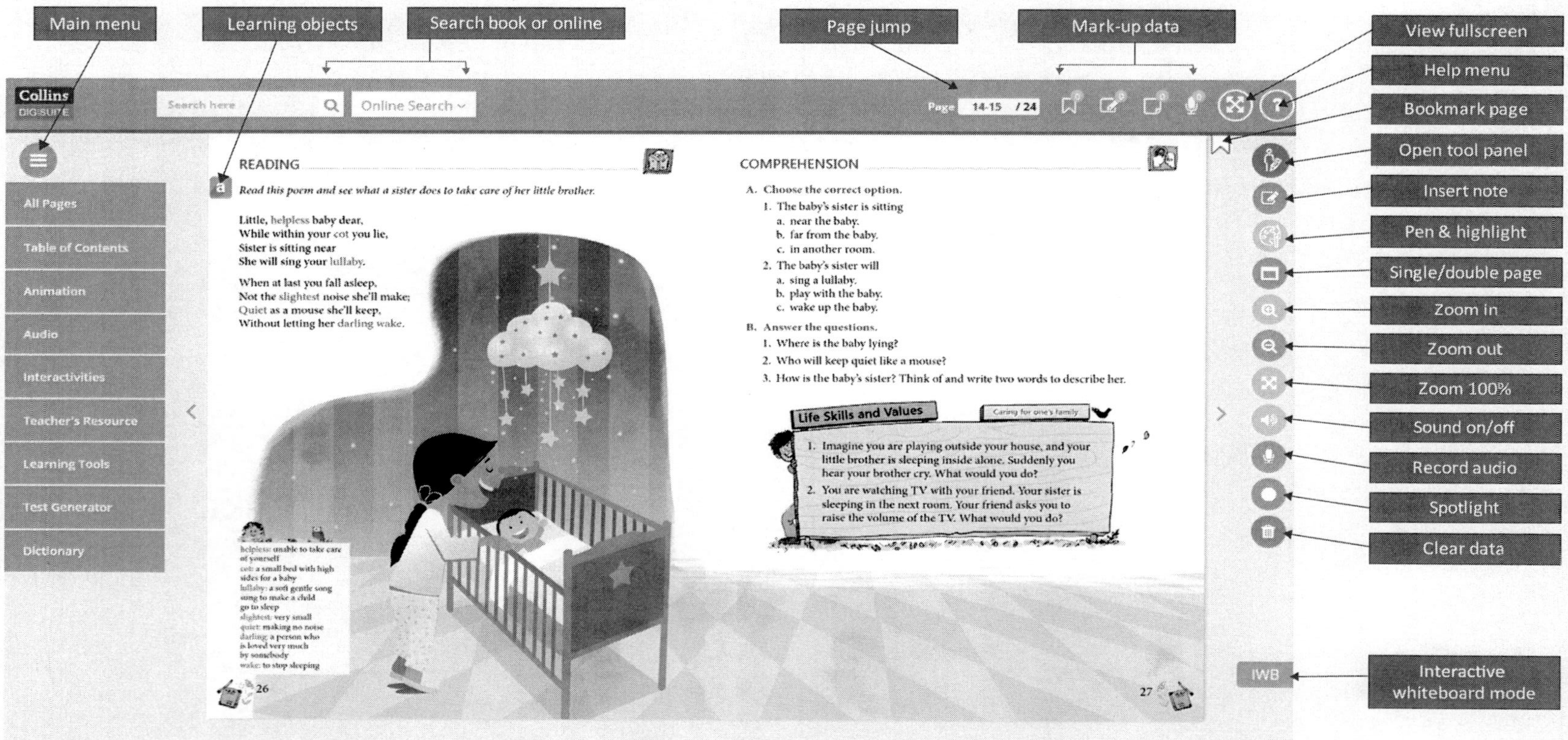

Student + Teacher

- **a** animations
- **ilt** instructor-led tutorials
- **ia** activities
- **w** worksheets
- audio
- **g** games
- **v** videos

Teacher-only

- **lp** lesson plans
- **w** worksheets
- **tn** teacher's notes
- **ak** answer keys

Preface

***Excursions* Revised Edition** is a comprehensive course in Environmental Studies and Social Studies for young learners. This series for classes 1 to 8 is aligned with the guidelines given in the National Education Policy, 2020. Following the curriculum, this series offers a course in Environmental Studies for classes 1 and 2, integrated Social Studies for classes 3, 4 and 5 and separate Geography and History and Civics courses for classes 6, 7 and 8. The series offers features that focus on essential skills to assist learners achieve holistic learning through a multidisciplinary approach.

The Integrated Social Studies course covers a wide range of concepts drawn from History, Civics and Geography. It deals with the study of social relationships and the functioning of society, equipping students with the knowledge and understanding of the past, necessary for coping with the present and planning for the future. It helps students affirm their place in an inclusive society. The engaging content develops social, cultural and analytical skills required to adjust to an increasingly interdependent and interconnected world.

In line with the new syllabus, the series follows a thematic and structured approach. The course material provides activities for cross-curricular linkages to connect learning across subject areas. Based on an interactive pedagogy, the books promote learning through inferential and experiential tasks and stimulating content. The series provides ample scope for the learners to observe, reflect, hone their thinking skills and develop effective communication skills.

Excursions Teachers' Manuals provide a comprehensive teaching aid to facilitate learning outcomes. Many skill-based activities have been suggested for the teachers to make teaching more interactive.

Key Features

- **Syllabus:** Latest syllabus prescribed by the CICSE
- **Period Plan:** Period wise lesson plans for each chapter
- **Lesson Plans:** Detailed lesson plans for each chapter
- **Answer Key:** Detailed answers to all the questions in the book
- **Additional Worksheet:** Additional worksheet for every chapter
- **Worksheet Key:** Answers to the additional worksheets

Syllabus

Theme 1: Evolution of Mankind		
Key Concepts/ Concerns	**Suggested Transactional Processes**	**Suggested Learning Resources**
• **Evolution of mankind:** – Brief introduction of story of Human evolution on earth – Sources/evidences (fossils, bones, utensils, cave paintings, tools, etc.) • **The four stone ages:** – Paleolithic – Mesolithic – Neolithic – Chalcolithic • **Iron age** • **Evolution of Transport and Communication:** – Invention of the wheel and beginning of transport. – Reaching distant places. – Trade and voyages. – Modern means of transport. – Need for writing. – Use of pigeons – Invention of telephone and telegraph – Printing press, – Computers – Satellites	• Discussing and mind mapping to explain the sources of evidence to trace human evolution. • Providing information about the four stone ages and the iron age through videos and PPTs followed by discussions. • Collecting information using digital media on the evolution of mankind and on early archaeological sites in India. • Arranging a visit to a museum and to an archaeological site followed by a class discussion. • Comparing and contrasting means of transport through the ages • Discussing and analysing how the evolution of transport and physical features of a place helped trade and commerce to flourish. • Showing videos and/or displaying books about famous voyages. • Discussing the evolution of communication and depicting this through a timeline (from pigeons to satellites). • Making a Power Point Presentation on the four Stone age and Iron age. ***<u>Organising Activity:</u>*** – Making a chart by groups of children to depict the sources of evidence to trace evolution of mankind. • Role play: – On the life of early men. – On *Gulliver's Travel* • Guest Lectures: – Inviting a historian and discuss – How do we trace history through archaeological sources? • Debate and discussion on the life before the invention of printing press.	• Collecting information from digital media. • Videos and PPTs. • Pictures and documentaries on early man. • Clay Tablets and sticks to write with. • Videos on archaeological sites. • Old newspapers for making homemade paper. • Flashcards, pictures and charts showing buildings and monuments. • Amar Chitra Katha. • Videos and books on famous voyages. • Guest lecture
Integration: Arts Education, Science, Languages		
Life Skill: Sharing, working in groups, leadership		

<table>
<tr><th colspan="3">Theme 2: The Constitution of India – Basic features</th></tr>
<tr><th>Key Concepts/ Concerns</th><th>Suggested Transactional Processes</th><th>Suggested Learning Resources</th></tr>
<tr><td>◆ The Indian Constitution (formation, nature, need, and guiding principles).
◆ Fundamental Rights and Duties.
◆ Basic features of the democratic form of government.
◆ Importance of Elections.
◆ Responsibilities
◆ of a citizen in a
◆ democratic polity.</td><td>◆ Showing the school almanac to explain the concept of the Constitution.
◆ Discussing and mind mapping to explain the nature, need, formation, and guiding principles of guiding constitution.
◆ Compiling a list of children's rights and duties in school and at home. This can be followed by giving them information on Fundamental Rights and Duties.
◆ Conducting a class debate on rights and duties to make children aware of the 'Fundamental Rights and Duties.'
◆ Facilitating a class discussion on the hierarchical structure in school to explain the structure of the Government of India.
◆ Acquiring knowledge through books, internet and encyclopaedias about the different types of government in the world.
Organising Activities
– Asking children to read the school Almanac and conduct a debate/quiz on the rules followed in the school.
– Draw a chart or make a power point presentation to show the structure of the Government of India.
– Conducting a class election to let the children have a hands-on experience of the steps and importance of a free and fair election.</td><td>◆ Hands-on experiences.
◆ School Almanac.
◆ Class elections
◆ Drawing a chart
◆ Reference Books
◆ Internet
◆ Encyclopaedia
◆ Audio visual aids.</td></tr>
<tr><td colspan="3">Integration: Languages</td></tr>
<tr><td colspan="3">Life Skill: Interpersonal skills, cooperation and leadership qualities</td></tr>
</table>

<table>
<tr><th colspan="3">Theme 3: The Earth – Its Geographical Features</th></tr>
<tr><th>Key Concepts/ Concerns</th><th>Suggested Transactional Processes</th><th>Suggested Learning Resources</th></tr>
<tr><td>◆ Locating places on the Earth:
– Latitudes (introduction, characteristics, important latitudes).
– Longitudes (introduction, characteristics).</td><td>◆ Using maps and the globe to understand and locate the important latitudes and longitudes.
◆ Explaining and facilitating children to find the difference in time zones.
◆ Studying the globe understanding and locating the three major temperature zones.
◆ Showing videos and /or diagrams to explain the temperature zones.</td><td>◆ Personal experiences of children.
◆ News clippings on weather report.
◆ Globe and maps, Digital globe
◆ Web sources</td></tr>
</table>

• Weather and Climate: – Difference between the weather and climate. – Factors that affect climate of a place. • Solar and Lunar Eclipse • Major temperature zones of the Earth: – Torrid – Temperature – Frigid	• Providing opportunities to children to share their personal experiences related to different weather and climates. • Asking questions and facilitating discussion related to likes and dislikes about various weather conditions. • Discussing on the factors that affect the climate of a place with examples. • Discussing with diagrams the solar and lunar eclipses. • Project work on the reasons that affect the climate of a place. • Case study on the climate of a particular place. • Collecting news clippings or TV reports on weather for a week and preparing a comprehensive report on it. • Guest lecture by a specialist on making a weather forecast.	• Charts and posters, models, diagrams, etc. • Newspaper clippings. • Project work. • Case studies. • Guest lectures.

Theme 4: India – A Diverse Country

Key Concepts/ Concerns	Suggested Transactional Processes	Suggested Learning Resources
• India: Location and extent • India and its neighbouring countries. • Climate of India (Different Seasons) – Summer season – Winter season – Rainy (Monsoon) season • Natural vegetation – Tropical evergreen – Deciduous (monsoon forest) – Thorn and Scrub – Montane forest	• Identifying and locating neighbouring countries of India on the World map. • Comparing the size and extent of India with other countries. • Discussing different types of climate in India and comparing the life of people living there. • Discussing with reasons about the varied climatic conditions in different parts of the country. • Preparing a project report by groups of children or individually on the climatic conditions of a place with reasons. • Showing Videos and/ or PPTs on different types of natural vegetation in different geographical conditions in the country. ***<u>Organising activities</u>*** – Making charts/posters on conservation of natural vegetation. – Encouraging children to collect/write poems/ songs on different seasons in India. – Making charts or posters on different types of trees and plants.	• Personal experiences. • Wall maps of the world, India – Political and Physical. • Models and charts on different types of vegetation. • Audio-visual materials and web sources. • Poems and songs.
Integration: Science		
Life Skill: Environmental conservation, empathy.		

Theme 5: The Environment – Major Concerns		
Key Concepts/ Concerns	**Suggested Transactional Processes**	**Suggested Learning Resources**
• Components of the Environment (biotic and abiotic). • Interdependence of and between different regions of the world. • Impact of local events on global environment, global warming, • Natural disasters: – Earthquake, – Cyclones, – Floods, – Droughts, – Volcanic eruptions, – Landslides • Effects and Precautions of natural disasters.	• Showing PPTs/videos and encouraging discussions on the components of environment • Discussions on how do people living in different regions depend on each other. • Providing opportunities to enlist biotic and abiotic components of the environment. • Creating situation to analyse various reasons for global warming. • Showing videos and sensitising on harmful impacts of global warming • Discussing precautions to be taken at the time of natural disasters. ***Organising activities*** • Encouraging to prepare charts and writing slogans on global warming. • Organising mock drills on natural disasters and related safety measures. • Collecting newspaper clippings on natural disasters and writing report on it. • Motivating children to take a pledge to plant trees and not burst crackers. • Conducting cleanliness drive • **Role Play:** – Performing Street plays to educate the masses about the effects of pollution	• Classroom discussions • Narratives and life experiences. • Newspapers, magazines, journals, charts, posters. • Audio-visuals and web sources. • Charts and Slogans. • Mock drills. • Role Play. • Tree Plantation.
Integration: Languages		
Life Skill: Awareness on Environmental concerns		

Theme 6: Natural Resources		
Key Concepts/ Concerns	**Suggested Transactional Processes**	**Suggested Learning Resources**
• Meaning of resources. • Renewable and Non-Renewable resources. • Renewable resources –(air, water, soil, plants, animals, solar energy and wind energy) – brief description.	• Providing opportunities to children to share their experiences with peers and discuss about various aspects in the theme. • Facilitating class discussion on the term resources and providing examples. • Providing facilities to identify and enlist various resources they see around them. • Providing opportunities in groups /individually to observe and discuss the differences between renewable and non-renewable resources.	• Pictures, charts and models. • PPTs and Videos. • Guest Lecturers. • Coal, petroleum, different minerals etc.

• Non-Renewable resources – (Coal and Petroleum, Minerals) – brief description.	• Assigning project work to children on causes and the importance /necessity to conserve our resources. • Inviting experts to talk on the theme and discuss issues with children. • Organising a role play session on life without petroleum resources. • Writing poems on the benefits of Nature (the sun, water, soil, plants etc.) in enriching our lives. • Exploring and enlisting ways to conserve different resources.	
Integration: Languages		
Life Skill: Conservation of natural resources		

Theme 7: Major Occupations in India

Key Concepts/ Concerns	Suggested Transactional Processes	Suggested Learning Resources
• **Agriculture:** – Types of crops, Food Crop, cash crop, – Development of agriculture, – Livestock rearing (map work). • **Industries:** – Major industries in India. – Large scale industries and small scale industries. – Other industries.	• Providing opportunities to children to share their personal observations on various forms of occupations. • Facilitating class discussions to provide opportunities to children to ask questions and narrate experiences on agriculture being the main occupation in India. • Discussing old and new methods of cultivation in agriculture. • Facilitating work in small groups for children to observe and compare the difference between a raw and a finished product. • Showing samples of cash crops and food crops and narrating differences between them. • Visiting to a field and interaction with the farmer. • Taking children to a field and interacting with a farmer on soil, crops methods and income through cultivation, issues and hardships faced by them • Providing opportunities to observe, identify and classify man-made and machine made things. • Discussing the role of industries in our life. • Collecting news /information on major industries in India and analysing the same. • Taking children to local artisans or a crafts mela and organising their interaction / discussion with the crafts person. • Taking children to an industry and discussing the various processes in the industry. • Visiting to an industry, interaction with workers and observing various processes. • Visiting to local artisans or a crafts mela.	• Children's personal experiences. • Samples of different crops. • Collection of Raw and Finished products. • Local Artisans / Farmers/People involved in other occupations.
Integration: Languages		
Life Skill: Conservation of natural resources		

Period Plan

Chapter	Periods	Period break-up
1. Evolution of Human Beings	7	Period 1: Introduction through general discussion and digital media
		Period 2: To read the chapter and complete Life Skills and Values activity
		Period 3: To recapitulate the chapter
		Period 4: Think Box and Picture Study
		Period 5: To complete the DIY activity
		Period 6: To assess learning outcomes
2. The Stone Age	10	Period 1: To show an introductory PowerPoint presentation to the students about the early humans followed by a discussion
		Period 2: To help the students understand how early humans communicated using gestures and signs
		Period 3: To explain the periodization of the Stone Age based on the types of tools used in each period
		Period 4: To dicuss the main features of the Palaeolithic Age
		Period 5: To talk about the discovery of fire during the Palaeolithic Age
		Period 6: To discuss the main features of the Mesolithic Age
		Period 7: To discuss the main features of the Neolithic and the Chalcolithic ages
		Period 8: To recapitulate the chapter
		Period 9: To assess learning outcomes
3. The Iron Age	10	Period 1: Introduction through word-building
		Period 2: To complete the warm-up activity and introduce the Bronze Age to the using ppt
		Period 3: To talk about the Iron Age to the students
		Period 4: To discuss the important developments of the Iron Age
		Period 5: To recapitulate the chapter
		Period 6: To assess learning outcomes
		Period 7: To complete the DIY activity
		Period 8: To make an Iron Age timeline in the class
		Period 9 and Period 10: To complete Enjoy

Chapter	Periods	Period break-up
4. Evolution of Transport and Communication	10	Period 1: To introduce the lesson with the help of a warm-up activity
		Period 2 and Period 3: Use ppt to explain the beginning of transport and famous voyages
		Period 4: To talk about the.......engine and its impact. The invention of the steam engine
		Period 5: To talk about the means of communication used during the ancient times
		Period 6: To discuss the developments made in the field of communication and modern means of communication
		Period 7: To recapitulate the chapter
		Period 8: To complete Life Skills and Values and Enjoy activities
		Period 9: To assess learning outcomes
5. The Indian Constitution	7	Period 1: Introduction through oral discussion
		Period 2: To explain the framing of the Indian Constitution
		Period 3: To explain the significance and the meaning of the Preamble to the Indian Constitution
		Period 4: To recapitulate the chapter
		Period 5: To explain the importance of rules through a role play
		Period 6: To assess learning outcomes
		Period 7: To complete the
6. Fundamental Rights and Duties	8	Period 1: Introduction of rights and duties through a discussion
		Period 2 and Period 3: To explain fundamental rights to the students
		Period 4: To talk about the importance of the fundamental duties
		Period 5 and Period 6: To understand rights and duties through a writing task
		Period 7: To recapitulate the chapter
		Period 8: To assess learning outcomes
7. The Indian Democracy	9	Period 1: Introduction through a discussion and defining democracy
		Period 2: To explain the salient features of a democracy
		Period 3 and Period 4: To explain the functions of the legislature and the executive
		Period 5: To explain the functions of the judiciary
		Period 6: To recapitulate the chapter
		Period 7: To arrange a field trip to a high court or a lower court
		Period 8: To complete Life Skills and Values and Enjoy activities
		Period 9: To assess learning outcomes

Chapter	Periods	Period break-up
8. Locating Places on the Earth	8	Period 1: To explain coordinates with the help of a classroom and ppt
		Period 2: To define latitudes and name the important latitudes of the Earth
		Period 3: To define longitudes and name the important longitudes of the Earth
		Period 4: Recapitulate the chapter
		Period 5: To complete Life Skills and Values activity
		Period 6: To complete the Enjoy activity
		Period 7: To assess learning outcomes
9. Weather and Climate	8	Period 1: Discussion based on personal experience how weather varies from place to place
		Period 2 and Period 3: To define climate and factors that affect the climate of a region
		Period 4: To recapitulate the chapter
		Period 5: To answer the question in Think Box
		Period 6: To complete Picture Study, Life Skills and Values
		Period 7: To complete the activity in Enjoy
		Period 8: To assess learning outcomes
10. The Major Temperature Zones	9	Period 1: Introducing the lesson through a hands on activity
		Period 2: To Relate previous knowledge to the climate and vegetation of the Torrid Zone
		Period 3: To Relate the climate and vegetation of the Temperate Zone
		Period 4: To Relate to location the climate and vegetation of the Frigid Zone
		Period 5: Revise the features of the Frigid Zone through of a speaking activity
		Period 6: To complete the DIY and Life Skills and Values activity
		Period 7: To recapitulate the chapter
		Period 8: To assess learning outcomes
11. Eclipses	7	Period 1: Introducing the lesson with the help of a warm-up activity
		Period 2: To explain the concept of shadows with the help of an activity
		Period 3: To explain how a solar eclipse through ppt
		Period 4: To explain how a lunar eclipse through ppt
		Period 5: To recapitulate the chapter
		Period 6: To assess learning outcomes

Chapter	Periods	Period break-up
12. India and Its Neighbours	7	Period 1: To introduce the chapter with the help of using a political map of India
		Period 2 and Period 3: Reading the chapter
		Period 4: To recapitulate the chapter
		Period 5: To complete Picture Study and Life Skills and Values
		Period 6: To assess learning outcomes
		Period 7: To complete the activities in Enjoy
13. Climate of India	8	Period 1: To introduce the lesson with the help of a discussion
		Period 2 and Period 3: To explain the weather conditions during the major seasons of India
		Period 4: To explain the climatic regions of using a map of India
		Period 5: To make a season tree booklet in class
		Period 6: To recapitulate the chapter
		Period 7: To assess learning outcomes
14. Natural Vegetation of India	7	Period 1: To introduce the lesson with the help of a narrative
		Period 2: To Using a map show the location the vegetation found in tropical evergreen, monsoon and dry deciduous forests
		Period 3: To Relate to personal observation during travel the vegetation found in deserts, tidal and montane forests
		Period 4: To Discuss the importance of conserving forests
		Period 5: To recapitulate the chapter
		Period 6: To assess learning outcomes
15. Agriculture	9	Period 1: To introduce the lesson with the help of a talking about foods they eat
		Period 2 and Period 3: To name and explain the distribution of the major food crops of in relation to climate and soil and staple diets
		Period 4 and Period 5: To talk about the distribution of the major cash crops of India
		Period 6: To recapitulate the chapter
		Period 7: To assess learning outcomes
		Period 8: To discuss healthy and unhealthy food
16. Industries	7	Period 1: Talk about the machines used in homes
		Period 2: : To discuss how a final product is made using raw materials
		Period 3: To define large scale industries
		Period 4: To define small scale and cottage. Discuss the relation between local materials Factory visit.
		Period 5: To explain the causes and harmful effects of industrial pollution
		Period 6: To recapitulate the chapter
		Period 7: To assess learning outcomes

Chapter	Periods	Period break-up
17. Natural Resources	6	Period 1: To introduce the lesson through a discussion
		Period 2: To explain the importance of renewable resources
		Period 3: To explain the importance of non-renewable resources
		Period 4: To explain the threats to natural resources and the ways in which they can be conserved
		Period 5: To recapitulate the chapter
		Period 6: To assess learning outcomes
18. Our Environment	10	Period 1: To introduce the chapter with the help of a group activity
		Period 2: To explain the biotic and abiotic components of the environment
		Period 3 and Period 4: To make a booklet about the biotic and abiotic components of the environment
		Period 5: To define globalization and its relate to recent impacts.
		Period 6: To recapitulate the chapter
		Period 7: To complete the activities in Life Skills and Values and Enjoy
		Period 8: To assess learning outcomes
		Period 9: To make 'Save the Earth' posters
19. Natural Disasters	8	Period 1: To introduce the lesson with the help of a short activity
		Period 2: To read the chapter
		Period 3 and Period 4: To complete activities in Enjoy
		Period 5: To recapitulate the relate to recent disasters
		Period 6: To do a mock evacuation drill
		Period 7: To complete the activities in Think Box, Picture Study and Life Skills and Values
		Period 8: To assess learning outcomes

Contents

1 Evolution of Human Beings

LESSON PLAN

Total required: 7 periods **Textbook Reference:** Page 7 to 11

Every lesson is introduced using different strategies, namely a narrative, a story, an anecdote, a discussion, ppt. The learning outcomes are clearly defined in Let's learn about.
The weblinks given at the end of each chapter may be used to introduce a lesson/concept or at the end to the lesson for extended learning.
Multidisciplinary activities in the chapters and Across the Boundary pages are designed for individual, pair and group work involving research and application based learning.
The concept maps at the end of the book in Snap Recap section giving quick recap of the lesson are a teaching aid to reinforce learning taking learner away from the rut of rote learning.

Weblinks

For more information, visit

https://www.history.com/topics/pre-history/hunter-gatherers

Last accessed on 31/July/2020

Period 1

Introductory activity: Read out the following passage:

Sania's mother, is a scientist. She gifted her a red t-shirt on the World Earth Day, which is observed on 22 April, every year. The logo on the t-shirt was that of the 'Evolution of Humans'. It also had a slogan which said, 'March for Science'. Sania asked her mother what the logo and the slogan symbolized. Her mother told her about the role that science plays in our lives and the need to encourage research that gives us an insight into the life on the Earth. Just as the evolution of humans brought changes and progress in the human race, we should support scientific research that will add to the progress and development of the world.

Now, ask the following questions to the students:

- What is evolution of humans?
- Did the human race begin with dinosaurs or started with monkeys and apes?

Encourage the students to discuss the answers based on their previous knowledge of the human evolution. Refer to **Reflect** and have a discussion based on it.

Period 2

Read the chapter aloud.

Discussion: Discuss about the lives of the hunter-gatherers. How was it different from our lives? Let the students share their views with reference to the questions in **Life Skills and Values** in the classroom.

Period 3

Ask the students to read out the points in **In a Nutshell**. Randomly ask some students to explain what each line means and discuss the important points covered in the chapter.

Have the students read the question in **Figure Out** and help them answer it.

Read out the fact in **FactPedia**, research and find out relevant facts based on them.

Period 4

Ask the students to answer the question in **Think Box**. Read out the information in **Green Earth** and discuss its relevance to the chapter. Help the students complete the **Picture Study** and discuss the answers in the class.

Period 5

Fun activity: I am a Hominid

Draw a picture of an early human.

Writing task: Ask the students to write a few lines about their life as a hominid.

Period 6

For quick recall, refer to **Snap Recap**. Help the students to answer the questions in **Workout**. Have them sit in pairs and discuss the answers. Guide the children to decode the secret message in **Enjoy**.

Period 7

Pair work: Let the students work in pairs and design a time machine for an early human using empty boxes and bottle caps. Let them make a list of questions that they can ask the early humans.

2 The Stone Age

Total required: 10 periods

Textbook Reference: Page 12 to 18

LESSON PLAN

Weblinks

For more information, visit

https://www.history.com/topics/pre-history/stone-age

https://www.bbc.co.uk/bitesize/topics/z82hsbk/articles/z33487h

Last accessed on 31/July/2020

Period 1

Introductory activity: Prepare a PowerPoint presentation for the students recapitulating the previous chapter about the evolution of human beings. Ask the students to answer the question in **Reflect**.

Period 2

Group activity: Dumb charades

Divide the class into two groups. Ask each group to tell a message to the other group only through gestures and signs. Explain it to them that early humans used to communicate with gestures and sign languages. Thus, children enact an event with the help of sign language and gestures, almost like a game of dumb charades. Read out the fact in **FactPedia** and discuss it with the students.

Period 3

Timeline

Tell the students that the Stone Age can be divided into three periods based on the types of tools used in each period. Draw a timeline on the board to explain the division of the Stone Age into the Palaeolithic Age, the Mesolithic Age and the Neolithic Age.

Period 4

Research work

Help the students carry out research regarding the Palaeolithic Age. Tell them it lasted for about 20,000 years. Explain that the tools used by the humans during this period were made from stone. Also tell them that the first form of language developed during the Palaeolithic Age.

Classwork: Show images of some of the tools from the Palaeolithic Age and ask the students the uses of these tools.

Period 5

Explanation

Explain the events that lead to the discovery of fire. Tell the students that the early humans discovered fire accidentally by rubbing two stones together. Tell the students that it was one of the most remarkable discoveries made by the humans as it changed their lives.

Activity: Help the students draw a timeline of events that lead to the discovery of fire as mentioned in **DIY**. Ask the students to complete the **Picture Study**.

Period 6

Discussion: Discuss what marked Palaeolithic Age from the Mesolithic Age. Explain that the tools used were improved forms of the Palaeolithic tools and apart from stones, bones were used as spears, saws and arrows for hunting animals. Tell the students that agriculture started during the Mesolithic Age and humans transformed from being the hunter-gatherers to food producers. Ask the students to answer the question in **Figure Out**.

Period 7

Explain the human evolution during the Neolithic Age. Tell them that the Neolithic Age was marked by the use of polished stone tools.

Introductory activity

Show students video about the 'The Story of the Wheel'. They can watch them online too.

Explain that the invention of the wheel, the domestication of animals and the potter's wheel were some of the major achievements of the Neolithic Period.

Have the students answer the question in **Think Box**. Explain the main features of the Chalcolithic Age to the students. Read the information in **Green Earth**.

Period 8

Ask the students to read out the points in **In a Nutshell**. Randomly ask some students to explain what each line means and then follow it with a discussion on the important points covered in the chapter.

Craftwork: Using match sticks or wooden ice cream sticks, ask the students to make a raft used for transportation by early humans. They can stick this on paper and draw an early human standing on it. They can also draw scenery around it.

Period 9

For a quick revision refer to **Snap Recap**. Ask students to answer the questions in **Workout**. Have them sit in pairs and ask them to discuss the answers.

Group activity: Divide the class into four groups and have them do **Enjoy**.

Period 10

Group work: Research

Based on the three periods of the Stone Age, divide the class into three groups. Ask them to find out about the inventions, discoveries, clothes, food, tools, cave paintings and the advancement in human evolution during these three periods. Using clay or pebbles, ask the students make figures of an early human. Let them create scenes from the life of early human as visualised by them. Exhibit with proper labelling.

3 The Iron Age

Total required: 10 periods **Textbook Reference:** Page 20 to 24

Weblinks

For more information, visit

https://www.history.com/topics/pre-history/iron-age

https://www.bbc.co.uk/bitesize/topics/z82hsbk/articles/z8bkwmn

Last accessed on 31/July/2020

Period 1

Pair work: Ask the students to make a list of words that have the word 'iron' either in the beginning, in the end or in between. For example, iron vessels, ironmonger, ironmongery, Iron Age, irony, environ, environment and ironworker. The pair that comes up with the maximum number of 'iron' words will be the winners. Pick up a few words from the list and ask their meanings. Gradually, introduce Iron Age and encourage students to talk about it based on their previous knowledge. Ask them the following questions:

- What is the Iron Age? Why is it called so?
- What were the uses of iron?
- The discovery of iron was a turning point in the history of the world? Why do you think so?

Period 2

Ask the students to answer the question in **Reflect**. Read out the chapter and discuss the lives of the people during the Iron Age. How was it different from the lives of the hunter-gatherers? Ask the students to recall the features of the Chalcolithic Age from the previous chapter. Ask the students to answer the question in **Figure Out**.

Period 3

Discussion

Tell the students that the discovery or iron marked the beginning of the Iron Age. Discuss how the discovery of iron was a turning point in the history of the world. Explain how iron had advantages over other metals.

Read out the information in **Green Earth** and discuss it with the students. Ask the students to complete the **Picture Study**.

Period 4

Explain the important developments in agriculture, trade, occupations, warfare and transport to the students. Define the concept of kingship and explain how a powerful ruler was needed to bring in peace. Ask the students to answer the question in **Figure Out**. Ask the students to answer the question in **Think Box**.

Period 5

For a quick revision refer to **Snap Recap**. Ask students to answer the questions in **Workout**. Have them sit in pairs and ask them to discuss the answers.

Period 6

Ask the students to read out the points in **In a Nutshell**. Randomly ask some students to explain what each line means and then have a discussion on the important points covered in the chapter. Let the students share their views about the question in **Life Skills and Values**.

Period 7

Pair work: Ask the students to collect pictures for **DIY** activity. The students can be asked to collect the pictures in advance to complete the activity. Provide the materials needed to complete the activity.

Writing task: The students should label the artefacts and write their uses.

Period 8

Extension activity

Iron Age Timeline: Join strips of paper for the students and fold and divide them into three segments—the Stone Age, the Bronze Age and the Iron Age. Ask them to make a timeline based on the kinds of tools used during these periods.

Periods 9 and 10

Group work

Have the students do the **Enjoy** activities together. Let the children paste or draw pictures and design an Iron Age granary. From the granary, they should show how grains were carried to the market place for selling. This should be substantiated with proper labelling.

4 Evolution of Transport and Communication

Total required: 10 periods

Textbook Reference: Page 25 to 33

Weblinks

For more information, visit

https://kids.nationalgeographic.com/explore/history/wright-brothers/

https://www.forbes.com/sites/solrogers/2019/10/15/the-role-of-technology-in-the-evolution-of-communication/#4733b770493b

https://www.history.com/topics/inventions/telegraph

Last accessed on 31/July/2020

Period 1

Introductory activity

Read out the following passage in the classroom:

Jason's family is from Port Blair and they love visiting it. Mostly, they travel to Port Blair on a ship. This year too, his family is planning to go for a holiday to Port Blair and Jason's father is looking up for cruise liners! "Oh, what fun it would be to travel in a cruise liner! ", said Jason. Jason wondered how his forefathers had travelled. He flipped through the pages of the old family album.

Jason brought the album to school to show it to his friends. Let us look at this album.

- Show different pictures of ancient and modern ships to the students.
- Ask the students how has transport changed over years?
- Ask them what do they think has lead to this change?

Discuss it with the students and talk about the famous voyages and explorers.

Periods 2 and 3

Help the students answer the questions in **Reflect**. Explain how early humans started using transport instead of walking or riding on animals. Explain how the invention of wheel revolutionized transportation.

Extended activity

Show a **power point presentation** or a video to the students about the European explorers who made long voyages during the 13th and the 14th centuries.

Period 4

Discussion

Discuss how the steam engine was the key invention that revolutionized the transport system. Explain the contribution of inventors such as Thomas Newcomen and James Watt. Tell the students about the invention of the first aircraft by Wilbur and Orville Wright. Discuss the improvements made in transport during the 20th century.

Ask the students to answer the question in **Figure Out**.

Period 5

Explain how sign language helped the early humans communicate. Tell them about the paintings found at archaeological sites across the world. Tell the students that the evidence for the first form of writing was found in Mesopotamia. Explain what are hieroglyphics and hieroglyphs. Read out facts in both the **FactPedia** and discuss it with the students. Have the students answer the question in **Figure Out**.

Extended learning: The Story of Letters

Ask the students to collect an old post card, inland letter, air mail and a telegram and write a few lines about them.

Writing task: The students can write short paragraphs about topics such as 'I am a Letter' or 'Life of an Old Postcard'.

Group activity: Divide the class into groups and help them design the hieroglyphs and write a secret message using these signs.

Period 6

Explain how the invention of the printing press by Johannes Gutenberg in 1440 was the turning point in the field of communication and how it revolutionized communication. Define mass communication. Read out the fact in **FactPedia**. Have the students make a list of the inventions that changed the world of communication. Discuss the modern means of communication such as computers, smartphones, and fax machines. Read out the information in **Green Earth**.

Homework: Ask the students to complete **DIY**.

Period 7

Ask the students to read the points in **In a Nutshell**. Randomly ask some students to explain each point and then discuss it with others.

Ask the students to answer the question in **Think Box** and complete the **Picture Study**.

Period 8

Ask the students to answer the questions in **Life skills and Values**. Guide the students to work on the word search given in **Enjoy**.

Role-play activity: Arrange a role-play in the class, a few students can participate in it. Provide role-play cards to each participant. The cards should clearly mention their acting out suggestions. Each participant will play the role of a newspaper reader, a person who loves watching television, a fax machine controller, a mobile phone lover and a book lover. The should be informed in advance that the role-play should bring out the importance of the means of communication.

Period 9

For a quick revision refer to **Snap Recap**. Ask students to answer the questions in **Workout**. Have them sit in pairs and ask them to discuss the answers.

Period 10

Group activity: Divide the class into four groups. Give each group chart paper. Ask two groups to work on any four the important inventions made in the field of transport and the other two groups work on the important inventions made in the field of communication. Ask the students to make a pictorial timeline about the changes that took place in the fields of transport and communication with appropriate labelling and display it in the classroom.

5 The Indian Constitution

Total required: 7 periods **Textbook Reference:** Page 35 to 40

Weblinks

For more information, visit

https://www.india.gov.in/my-government/constitution-india

Last accessed on 31/July/2020

Period 1

Introductory activity: Begin the class by asking the following questions:

- Why is 26 January an important date in India?
- Why do we celebrate the Republic Day on this date?
- Why did the Indian Constitution come into effect on 26 January?
- What do you mean by the Republic of India?
- What was the need of having a written constitution?
- Who wrote the Constitution of India?

Refer to **Reflect**. Encourage the students to answer independently. A supporting **PowerPoint presentation** can also be shown to the class. Brief the students about the importance of rules.

Period 2

Explain why there was a need for framing a constitution after gaining independence from the British and link it to the need for rules in school in a classroom. Provide a brief background about the Constituent Assembly and why it was formed. Tell the students why the Republic Day is celebrated.

Extended activity

A short clip of Republic Day celebration may be shown to the students. Read out the fact in **FactPedia** and give examples of the features borrowed from other constitutions of the world. Ask the students to answer the question in **Figure Out**. Explain the nature of the Indian Constitution. Ask them to read the fact in **FactPedia** and find out more about the leaders. Read out the information in **Green Earth** and discuss it with the students.

Help the students answer the questions in **Think Box**.

Period 3

Talk to the students about the significance of the Preamble and explain why it was added to the Constitution. Randomly, select volunteers from the class and assign parts of the Preamble to them. Ask them to read out their portions in the class. After they have finished reading, explain the meaning and significance of words such as sovereign, socialist, secular, democratic, republic, justice, liberty, equality and fraternity with examples.

Ask the students to answer the question in **DIY**. Ask the students to complete the **Picture Study**.

LESSON PLAN

Period 4

Ask the students to read points in **In a Nutshell**. Randomly ask some students to explain what each point and discuss it with their classmates. Ask the students to share their views with reference to **Life Skills and Values**.

Period 5

Role play: Arrange a role play in which the teacher gives a situation to a group of students, 'A Day without Any Rules'. Divide the class into 5 to 6 groups. Give chits with different situations written on them.

Examples:

- A school without any fixed rules
- Not obeying rules on the road

Period 6

For a quick revision refer to **Snap Recap**. Ask students to answer the questions in **Workout** and ask them to sit in pairs and ask them to discuss the answers.

Period 7

Guide the students to complete the activities in **Enjoy**.

6 Fundamental Rights and Duties

Total required: 8 periods **Textbook Reference:** Page 41 to 45

Weblinks

For more information, visit

https://www.india.gov.in/topics/law-justice

Last accessed on 31/July/2020

Period 1

Introductory activity: Begin the class by discussing the following question with the students:

Suppose one day, a rule is passed that all educational institutions will be shut for an indefinite period of time.

What will be your reaction?

- Encourage the students to voice their opinions.
- Introduce the topic of rights and duties. Tell the students that according to the Indian Constitution, every person has the right to get proper education and it is our duty to go to the educational institutions.
- Show a few more examples to explain the differences between rights and duties.

Ask the students to answer the question in **Reflect**.

Periods 2 and 3

Explain the fundamental rights enshrined in the Constitution of India to the Indian citizens. Read out the fact in **FactPedia**. Explain the cultural and educational rights to the students. Read out the information in **Green Earth** and explain its relevance to the students. Ask the students to answer the question in **Figure Out**. Ask the students complete the **Picture Study**.

Homework: Ask the students to answer the questions in **Think Box**.

Period 4

Read out the fundamental duties to the students. Ask the students to answer the questions in **Life Skills and Values**.

Periods 5 and 6

Writing task: My Right or My Duty?

Ask the students to make a booklet of fundamental rights and duties. Draw a picture that depicts a fundamental right. Ask the students to draw and write the corresponding duty. Similarly, draw a picture depicting a fundamental duty and ask the students to draw and write the corresponding right. As a reinforcement, the following exercise can be done at the end of the writing task:

Written Exercise

Read the sentences and write whether it is a fundamental 'duty' or a 'right'.

1. We should all try to stay healthy
2. All children must go to school till the age of 14 years
3. We should always stand whenever we sing or hear the National Anthem
4. We must try to keep our city clean
5. We should take care of our parents and respect them

Period 7

Quiz activity

Ask students to read the school almanac for homework. Conduct a quiz on it.

Ask the students to do the activity in **DIY**. Encourage the students to answer honestly. Ask the students to read the points **In a Nutshell**. Randomly ask some students to explain what each line means and then discuss the answers.

Period 8

For a quick revision refer to **Snap Recap**. Ask the students to answer the questions in **Workout**. Have them sit in pairs and ask them to discuss the answers.

Homework: Ask students to do the **Enjoy** activities at home, and bring it in the next class.

7 The Indian Democracy

Total required: 9 periods **Textbook Reference:** Page 46 to 53

LESSON PLAN

Weblinks

For more information, visit

https://www.india.gov.in/my-government/whos-who/members-parliament

Last accessed on 31/July/2020

Period 1

Introductory activity: Discuss the following questions with the students.

- How many states does India have? Do they have similar or different cultures?
- Do you think that there is a unifying bond amongst the people of India even though they belong to different backgrounds?
- What does it tell you about our country?

Ask leading questions and talk about democracy. Name a few democratic countries of the world.

Period 2

Begin the class by asking the students to answer the question in **Reflect**.

Discussion

Talk about a democracy and discuss the salient features. Explain the structure of a federal government and the distribution of power according to the union, the state and the concurrent lists. Tell the students that the Indian Governments, like most other governments, has three branches—the executive, the legislature and the judiciary. Ask the students to answer the question in **Figure Out**.

Research: Homework: Ask the students to find out details and complete the **DIY** activity.

Periods 3 and 4

Explain the division of the legislature into the Lok Sabha and the Rajya Sabha. Explain the functions of each and the functions of a speaker.

Tell the students about the process of an election in India. Tell them about political parties and constituencies. Explain the concept of a majority party and opposition. Read out the fact in **FactPedia.** Help the students to find out the answer to the question in **Figure Out**. Explain the functions of the executive.

Period 5

Explain the functions of the Indian judiciary. Tell the students about the importance of the Supreme Court.

Explain the importance of elections and responsibilities of a citizen. Ask the students to read the information in **Green Earth**.

Period 6

Ask the students to read the points **In a Nutshell**. Randomly ask some students to explain what each line means and ask them to discuss the answers. Ask the students to complete the exercise in **Think Box**.

Pair work: Based on **Picture Study**, have the students discuss and prepare a questionnaire for the councillor of the area about the difficulties faced by the people in the neighbourhood.

Period 7

Field Trip: Arrange a visit to a high court or other lower courts for the students to gain first-hand knowledge about how a court functions.

Writing task: Ask the students to write a short essay about their visit.

Period 8

Explain and guide the students to prepare a speech based on **Life Skills and Values** in class.

Role play: With reference to **Enjoy** help the students perform a mock election in class.

Period 9

For a quick revision refer to **Snap Recap**. Ask students to answer the questions in **Workout**. Have them sit in pairs and ask them to discuss the answers.

8 Locating Places on the Earth

Total required: 7 periods **Textbook Reference:** Page 54 to 60

Weblinks

For more information, visit

https://www.bbc.co.uk/bitesize/topics/zvsfr82/articles/zd4rmfr

https://www.nationalgeographic.org/encyclopedia/prime-meridian/?utm_source=BibblioRCM_Row

Last accessed on 31/July/2020

Period 1

Introductory activity: Draw a grid with five rows and five columns on a chart. Paste pictures, or write names of animals or birds in each box. Ask the students to write down the location of each animal with reference to the row and the column number. For example, the location of lion can be expressed as 'a1'. Likewise, the location of mouse can be expressed as '5b'. Tell the students that in a similar way the location of places on the Earth can be determined with the help of coordinates. Relate this exercise to latitudes and longitudes and show them a grid drawn on a globe. Draw their attention to the vertical and horizontal lines. Ask them if they have seen such lines together. If yes, where? Refer to maps and globes. The imaginary lines drawn across them are called latitudes and longitudes.

	1	2	3	4	5
a	lion		panda		toucan
b		Dog		horse	mouse
c		cat			frog
d	giraffe		tiger	deer	
e	elephant	sheep			squirrel

Now, refer to **Reflect** and let the students have fun locating the buildings.

Period 2

With the help of a globe, point out the Equator. Explain that the lines drawn on the globe, running parallel to the Equator are called latitudes. Explain the properties of latitudes and point out the Northern and the Southern hemispheres. Point out the important parallels of latitude on a globe. Read out the information in **FactPedia** and **Green Earth**. Ask the students to answer the question in **Figure Out**.

Extended Learning

Google Earth YouTube videos can be used to show 3D images.

Period 3

With the help of a globe, point out the Prime Meridian. Explain that the lines drawn to the east and west of the Prime Meridian are called longitudes. Explain the properties of the longitudes and point out the Eastern and the Western hemispheres. Point out the International Date Line on the globe. Read out the fact in **FactPedia**. Have the students complete the activity in **DIY**.

Period 4

Ask the students to read the points in **In a Nutshell**. Randomly ask some students to explain each point and then follow it with a discussion on the important points covered in the chapter. Ask the students to complete the exercises in **Think Box** and **Picture Study**.

Period 5

Extended learning

Divide the class into 4 to 5 groups. Tell them they are on a mission to find the hidden treasure on a Treasure Island but no one knows the exact location of this treasure. Have each group draw a treasure map that will help them to locate the treasure. While drawing the map, they have to consider the coordinates and the cardinal and ordinal directions.

Period 6

Group work: Have the students make a **PowerPoint presentation** as mentioned in **Enjoy**.

Period 7

For a quick revision refer to **Snap Recap**. Ask the students to do answer the questions in **Workout**. Have them sit in pairs and ask them to discuss the answers.

9 Weather and Climate

Total required: 8 periods **Textbook Reference:** Page 62 to 67

Weblinks

For more information, visit

https://www.nationalgeographic.com/science/earth/earths-atmosphere/climate/

https://climatekids.nasa.gov/climate-change-meaning/

Last accessed on 31/July/2020

Period 1

Introductory activity: Read this short passage.

Saba's cousin lives in Australia and she is coming to India to spend her winter holidays in Pune. It was the month of June and it had started snowing in Australia. Snowing? Saba wondered as it was hot and sultry in Pune. Saba decided to ask her class teacher the next day to understand the difference between the climate of different places.

Encourage the students to discuss the following questions.

- Why is the climate in the two places so different?
- In which hemisphere is Australia located?
- Do they know about the seasons in Australia?
- What is the difference between weather and climate?

Periods 2 and 3

Refer to **Reflect** and help the students complete the activity. Name the main seasons of India and explain the prevailing weather conditions during these seasons. Read the fact in **FactPedia**.

Explain the term climate to the students. Ask the difference and then tell them to read the difference between weather and climate as explained in the table. Explain the factors that affect the climate of a place.

Have the students answer the question in **Figure Out**. Ask the students to read the information on **Green Earth**. Read out the fact in **FactPedia**.

Homework: Ask the students to answer the question in **DIY**.

Period 4

Ask the students to read out the points in **In a Nutshell**. Randomly ask some students to explain what each line means and then follow it with a discussion on the important points covered in the chapter.

Extended learning

Using a paper plate and a pinwheel, ask the students to make a weather wheel. They can have fun guessing the day's weather and then predicting whether it is going to change or not.

Period 5

Ask the students to work with their partners and design a poster to generate awareness about global warming.

Period 6

Ask the students to do the **Picture Study**.

Role-play: Arrange a role-play based on the activity in **Life Skills and Values**.

Writing task: Ask students to write a passage about the changing seasons which can be displayed on the soft board.

Period 7

Group work: Help the students prepare a PowerPoint presentation as mentioned in **Enjoy** and present it in the class.

Period 8

For a quick revision refer to **Snap Recap**. Ask the students to answer the questions in **Workout**. Have them sit in pairs and ask them to discuss the answers.

10 The Major Temperature Zones

Total required: 8 periods **Textbook Reference:** Page 68 to 73

Weblinks

For more information, visit

https://www.natgeokids.com/au/home-is-good/savannah-habitat/#:~:text=Super%20habitat!,is%20warm%2C%20all%20year%20round!

https://kids.nationalgeographic.com/explore/nature/habitats/polar/

Last accessed on 30/July/2020

Period 1

Introductory activity: Show a globe to the students and ask them to describe what it is used for. Ask the questions such as:

- How does a globe help us?
- Which phenomenon takes place because of the tilt of the Earth's axis?
- Why are places near the Equator hotter than those located near the poles?
- What are temperature zones?

Ask the students to complete the activity in **Reflect**. Encourage the students to unscramble the words on their own. It can be done as a pair activity.

Period 2

Explain the location and extent of the Torrid Zone with the help of a map. Name the countries or parts of countries that are located in the Torrid Zone. Name the sub-regions of the Torrid Zone.

Explain the vegetation of the equatorial and the tropical region. Read out the fact in **FactPedia.**

Explain the climate and vegetation of the tropical grasslands and hot deserts.

Period 3

Explain the location and extent of the Temperate Zone with the help of a map. Name the regions of the world that are located in this zone. Read out the fact in **FactPedia**. Explain the wildlife and vegetation of the Temperate Zone. Read out the information in **Green Earth**.

Period 4

Explain the location and extent of the Frigid Zone with the help of a map. Name the regions of the world that are located in this zone. Explain the wildlife and vegetation of the Frigid Zone. Ask the students to answer the question in **Figure Out**. Explain the difference between the Northern and the Southern frigid zones with the help of the table. Ask the students to complete the **Picture Study**.

Period 5

Extended learning: Speaking activity

Ask the students to answer and discuss the following questions in pairs.

- Have you ever visited a place covered with snow?
- What did you do there?
- Did you play with snow or make a snow sculpture?
- Have you come across a character made of snow in any of the stories you have read?
- If you have the option, how will you make a snow sculpture of your choice?

Writing activity: Ask the students to write an imaginative paragraph about a character made of snow.

Reading activity: Ask the students to exchange and read aloud their partner's writing.

Period 6

Conduct the activities in **DIY** and **Life Skills and Values** together. Divide the class into two groups and assign the equatorial region to one group and frigid zone to the other. Ask them to follow the given rubrics and do the research work. Have them present their findings in the class.

Period 7

Ask the students to read the points in **In a Nutshell**. Randomly ask some students to explain what each line means and then follow it up with a discussion on the points covered. Ask the students to answer the questions in **Think Box**.

Period 8

For a quick revision refer to **Snap Recap**. Ask students to answer the questions in **Workout**. Have them sit in pairs and ask them to discuss the answers.

Homework: Ask the students to complete the activity in **Enjoy** and bring it to the next class.

11 Eclipses

Total required: 8 periods **Textbook Reference:** Page 74 to 79

LESSON PLAN

Weblinks

For more information, visit

https://spaceplace.nasa.gov/eclipses/en/

https://www.nasa.gov/audience/forstudents/5-8/features/nasa-knows/what-is-an-eclipse-58

Last accessed on 31/July/2020

Period 1

Introductory activity: Read out the following passage to the students:

Mr. Saleem, the geography teacher, was teaching the students about the solar and lunar eclipses. All his students were excited to know about them. The news also showed the prediction of an eclipse. Mr. Saleem brought a torch and a big and small ball to class. He labelled the torch as the Sun, the big ball as the Earth and the small ball as the Moon. Then, Mr. Saleem, asked one of the students to hold the Earth in hand while he held the Moon in front of the Earth. As he switched on the torch (rays of the Sun), and held it straight, the shadow of the small ball (the Moon) fell on the big ball (the Earth). The same phenomenon happens in the solar system also. When the shadow of the Moon falls on the Earth, it is known as a solar eclipse.

A similar experiment was conducted with the student now holding the small ball (the Moon) and Mr. Saleem holding the big ball (the Earth). As the torch is switched on, the big ball prevents any light from falling on the small ball. This is called lunar eclipse. After carrying out this activity ask the students to explain the differences between two eclipses. Ask simple questions related to eclipses as a reinforcement activity.

Ask the students to complete the activity in **Reflect**.

Period 2

Fun activity: Tell the students how shadows are formed. Select volunteers and ask them to make different shapes with their hands as mentioned in **DIY**. Ask them how they can make the shadows bigger or smaller.

Period 3

Explanatory activity

Draw the diagram of a solar eclipse on the board and tell the students how it occurs. Explain umbra and penumbra to the students. Tell the students how partial and total solar eclipses occur. Web links may be used to reinforce the concept. Ask the students to answer the question in **Figure Out**. Ask the students to find words related to eclipse given in the word grid in **Enjoy**.

Period 4

Draw the diagram of a lunar eclipse on the board and tell the students how it occurs. Explain how total and partial lunar eclipses occur. Read out the information in **Green Earth**.

Period 5

Ask the students to read the points in **In a Nutshell**. Randomly ask some students to explain what each line means and then follow it with a discussion on the important points covered in the chapter. Have the students complete the **Picture Study**.

Homework: Ask the students to complete the question in **Life Skills and Values** and bring it to the next class.

Period 6

For a quick revision refer to **Snap Recap**. Ask the students to answer the questions in **Workout**. Have them sit in pairs and ask them to discuss the answers.

Period 7

Read out the poem 'The Moon' by Robert Louis Stevenson

Extended learning

Encourage the students to make a pictorial dictionary of words associated with the Moon, spacecraft, craters, astronauts, planets and stars. It could also include new words such as weightless, gravity, adventure, and satellite. This can be followed by writing a short paragraph on, 'Being an Astronaut' or 'A Meeting with Aliens'.

12 India and Its Neighbours

Total required: 7 periods

Textbook Reference: Page 80 to 85

Weblinks

For more information, visit

https://mea.gov.in/india-and-neighbours.htm

https://kids.nationalgeographic.com/explore/countries/nepal/

Last accessed on 31/July/2020

Period 1

Introductory activity: Read out the following paragraph to the students:

Varun was excited about the football tournament that was to be held in Kolkata. His favourite team was going to play and his mother had bought tickets for it. Players from different countries such as India, Bangladesh, Sri Lanka, Australia, England and New Zealand would be participating in the tournament. Varun was happy that there was unity in diversity and all the players would play as one team. He eagerly waited for the day when he would be able to see his favourite players on the field.

Ask the students the following questions:

- Ask the students to locate the participating countries in their atlases.
- What is common to the first five countries mentioned on the paragraph?
- Ask them if they can find out the names of a few more neighbouring countries of India.
- Ask them if they have visited any of the neighbouring countries of India. If yes, encourage the students to talk about them and their experiences. Ask the students to answer the questions in **Reflect**.

Periods 2 and 3

Read out the chapter. Explain the location of the neighbouring countries of India with the help of a political map of India. The map can also be shown online or through a slide using MS paint to highlight the regions. Students can be involved in demonstrating and pointing. Ask students to answer the questions in **Figure Out**. Let them read the fact in **FactPedia** and explain its relevance to the chapter. Read out the fact in **FactPedia**.

Period 4

Ask the students to read the points in **In a Nutshell**. Randomly ask some students to explain each point and then follow it with a discussion on the important points covered in the chapter. Ask the students to answer the questions in **DIY**.

Research: Homework: Ask the students to find information about the SAARC countries as mentioned in **Think Box**.

Role-play: Based on the information collected for Think Box, ask the students to talk about the culture, dance, music and dresses of all the SAARC countries. Ask them to have a role play and explain the culture of the countries to each other.

Period 5

Explain and ask the students to do **Picture Study** and **Life Skills and Values** in class.

Period 6

For a quick revision refer to **Snap Recap**. Ask the students to answer the questions in **Workout**. Have them sit in pairs and ask them to discuss the answers.

Period 7

Extended learning

Handbook: Draw and colour the flags of India's neighbouring countries, related to **Enjoy**. Now, collect a few pictures of famous landmarks from the neighbouring countries of India and paste them under the respective country flag. Once completed, the handbooks can be displayed for others to see.

13 Climate of India

Total required: 7 periods **Textbook Reference:** Page 86 to 91

Weblinks

For more information, visit

https://knowindia.gov.in/profile/climate.php

https://kids.nationalgeographic.com

https://www.nationalgeographic.org/encyclopedia/monsoon/

Last accessed on 31/July/2020

Period 1

Introductory activity

Display a few weather symbols on the board and ask the students if they can identify them. Ask them the following questions:

- What do these symbols depict?
- Ask them where they have seen such symbols.
- What is the difference between weather and climate? Encourage them to discuss the different types of weather that is prevalent in the different seasons.
- What are the seasons that we find in India?

Ask the students to complete the activity in **Reflect**. Encourage them to answer independently and discuss the answers.

Periods 2 and 3

Explain the weather conditions that prevail during winter, summer, monsoon, spring and autumn. Explain the duration and temperature ranges during each season. Explain the temperature and pressure maps to the students. Help them connect it to the weather conditions of each season.

Group activity

Ask the students to answer the question in **Figure Out**. Let the students talk about the different places they have visited, compare the climate of a coastal area to a desert region or the mountains. They should give reasons for the difference in the climate.

Help the students to answer the question in **Think Box** and discuss the answers in the class.

Period 4

Map study

Name and point out the climatic regions of India on a physical map of India. Point out the states or parts of the states that are located in these climatic regions. Ask the students to answer the question in **Figure**. Read out the information in **Green Earth**.

Ask the students to complete the **Picture Study**.

Period 5

Extended learning

Season tree booklet: Ask the students to take card paper in four layers and cut them in the shape of a tree. Have them decorate the trees using colours.

Writing task: Ask the students to write down the characteristics of each season under the appropriate tree. Once complete, the booklets can be displayed for others to refer to.

Homework: Ask the students to write a report as mentioned in **Life Skills and Values** and bring it to the next class.

Period 6

Ask the students to read the points in **In a Nutshell**. Randomly ask some students to explain each point and then follow it with a discussion.

Pair work: Ask the students to complete **DIY**. Explain how to read the bar graphs and answer the questions.

Homework: Ask the students to do the activity in **Enjoy** and bring it to the next class.

Period 7

For a quick revision refer to **Snap Recap**. Ask the students to answer the questions in **Workout**. Have them sit in pairs and ask them to discuss the answers.

Individual activity

Little Chefs at Work: Encourage the students to make a sweet and a savoury dish at home, popular during their favourite season and share it with their friends the next day.

14 Natural Vegetation of India

Total required: 6 periods

Textbook Reference: Page 92 to 97

Weblinks

For more information, visit

http://www.forest.kerala.gov.in/index.php/forest/forest-types

http://moef.gov.in/forest-wildlife/forest-3/

Last accessed on 31/July/2020

Period 1

Introductory activity

Read out the following passage in the class:

Ayan was looking forward to the Christmas holidays as his family was planning a road trip from the north to the south of India. He was very excited as he was studying about the natural vegetation of India and wanted to see how it changed with the different landforms that they would be passing through. Ayan quickly opened his atlas to see the page on natural vegetation of India and glanced through the different types of vegetation found in India. He made a note of the states and their natural vegetation in his small diary.

- Show the students a map of the natural vegetation of India. Let the students identify the states and their natural vegetation. (Refer to **Enjoy**)
- Ask the students if they can point out what kind of vegetation will Ayan be seeing?
- Tell them about the different types of natural vegetation found in India.

Ask the students to look at the images in **Reflect** and complete the activity.

Period 2

Discuss the vegetation found in the tropical evergreen forests. Name the trees that grow here. Explain the difference between the deciduous and dry deciduous forests. Point out the regions of India that have this type of vegetation.

Pair work: With reference to the question in **Life Skills and Values** ask the students to describe the natural vegetation and wildlife of their native states.

Period 3

Discuss the vegetation found in the deserts. On the map point out the regions of India that have this type of vegetation. Name the trees and plants that are found in tidal forests and point out the regions in India where they are found. Similarly, name the trees and plants that are found in montane forests. Read out the fact in **FactPedia**. Web links and teacher made PPT will show the students real life images of the vegetation. Ask the students to complete the **Picture Study**.

Homework: Ask the students to complete the activity in **Enjoy**. Arrange the leaves in such a manner that they form different animal figures. Display these on a soft board.

Period 4

Explain why the conservation of forests is important. Read out the information in **Green Earth**. Ask the students to answer the question in **Figure Out**.

Group activity: Ask the students to complete the activity in **DIY**. Help them read the graph and then answer the questions.

Map skills

On an outline map of India, show the students how to mark the main forest types found in India as given in the **Map Work** activity.

Period 5

Ask the students to read the points in **In a Nutshell**. Randomly ask some students to explain each point means and then follow it with a discussion on the important points covered in the chapter.

Period 6

For a quick revision refer to **Snap Recap**. Ask students to answer the questions in **Workout**. Have them sit in pairs and ask them to discuss the answers.

15 Agriculture

Total required: 9 periods **Textbook Reference:** Page 98 to 106

Weblinks

For more information, visit

https://www.nationalgeographic.org/encyclopedia/crops/

https://megagriculture.gov.in/PUBLIC/crops_food_grains.aspx

Last accessed on 31/July/2020

Period 1

Introductory activity

Food Festival: The senior students of Harbour Front Centre were organising a food festival based on the staple food of different states of India. As the children walked through the school gate, they saw a huge banner put up near the entrance. Hot aloo parathas, *makai ki roti*, idli, crispy dosas, yummy poha, *besan ka chilla* and fried rice were on the menu. The list was never ending. The best part of the food festival was that the money collected would go to an old people's home

Ask the students following questions:

- What do they think of when they see such a banner?
- What is staple food?
- What is the staple food of the state they belong to?
- Name the different types of crops grown in India.

Based on **brainstorming and discussion**, introduce the topic of agriculture to the students. Now refer to **Reflect** and ask the students to unscramble the words.

Periods 2 and 3

Tell the students the definition of food crops. Explain the growing conditions of rice. On a map point out the rice producing regions of India. Explain the growing conditions of wheat. On a map, point out the major wheat producing regions of India. Read out the information in **Green Earth**. Similarly, explain the growing conditions and distribution of major cereals, pulses, sugarcane and oilseeds in India.

Homework: Ask the students to answer the question in **Think Box** and bring it to the next class.

Periods 4 and 5

Tell the students the definition of cash crops. Explain the growing conditions of tea and coffee. On a map point out the major coffee and tea producing regions of India. Ask the students to answer the question in **Figure Out** and read the fact in **Factpedia**. Explain the growing conditions major production regions of jute, cotton, tobacco and rubber. Ask the students to complete the **Picture Study**.

Homework: Ask the students to complete the activity in **Enjoy**.

Period 6

Ask the students to read the points in **In a Nutshell**. Randomly ask some students to explain each point and follow it with a discussion on the important points covered in the chapter. Ask the students to do **DIY** in class.

Period 7

Group activity

Scrapbook: Ask the students to choose any four states of India, from the north, south, east and west. Collect pictures of the crops cultivated in these states and the dishes made out of the staple food. At the end, they can write down a recipe in which those cereals or grains have been used.

Period 8

For a quick revision refer to **Snap Recap**. Ask students to answer the questions in **Workout**. Have them sit in pairs and discuss the answers.

Period 9

Extended learning

- Have the students write the names of four crops and the different types of food made from them.
- Ask them to collect a few wrappers/packets and note down the ingredients used, nutritional value, date of manufacture, expiry date, and name of the company that makes the product.
- Initiate a discussion about healthy and junk food.
- Ask the students why we should not eat food that is past its expiry date?

Encourage each student to discuss their opinions.

16 Industries

Total required: 7 periods **Textbook Reference:** Page 107 to 112

LESSON PLAN

Weblinks

For more information, visit

https://www.india.gov.in/topics/industries

https://greentribunal.gov.in/

Last accessed on 31/July/2020

Period 1

Introductory activity

Show photos of a few industrialized regions of the world. Based on them ask questions to the students in the form of an oral comprehension. Ask them the following questions:

- What does this picture tell you?
- Ask leading questions about industrialisation, manufacturing, employment, empowerment, growth of a region.
- Discuss the kind of raw materials used to run industries, what happens to the final products and how they reach the markets.
- What are the positive and negative impacts of industrialisation?
- How does industrialization affect the environment?
- What steps can be taken to reduce the negative impacts industrialization?

Period 2

Using the questions given in **Reflect** ask the students for their opinions on how a final product is manufactured using the raw materials. Examples of products such as notebooks, or food product can be used. Provide materials needed for doing the activity in **DIY**. After the activity is complete ask the students if they can write a short paragraph about the making of the candles using the raw materials that were provided to them.

Period 3

Define a large scale industry to the students. Give some examples of large scale industries in India. Point out the major industrial belts with the help of the map. Students can read out the fact in **FactPedia**. Help the students answer the question in **Think Box**.

Period 4

Tell the students about the small scale industries found in India. Explain the importance of the cottage industries. Explain how the cottage industry contributes to the economy of villages and small towns.

Period 5

Explain how industrialization causes pollution. Read out the information in **Green Earth** and explain the responsibilities of the Central Pollution Control Board of India. Briefly tell the students about clean fuel. Ask the students to complete the **Picture Study**.

Period 6

Ask the students to read the points in **In a Nutshell**. Randomly ask some students to explain each point and follow it with a discussion on the important points covered in the chapter.

Group activity: Divide the class into groups of four and help the students to find out information about a factory located near the school. If possible, take the students on a visit to a nearby factory or manufacturing unit, a craft mela, a cottage industry for a real life experience. Complete the exercise in **Enjoy**.

Period 7

For a quick revision refer to **Snap Recap**. Ask the students to answer the questions in **Workout**. Have them sit in pairs and ask them to discuss the answers.

17 Natural Resources

Total required: 6 periods **Textbook Reference:** Page 114 to 119

LESSON PLAN

Weblinks

For more information, visit

https://climatekids.nasa.gov/carbon/

https://www.nationalgeographic.org/encyclopedia/renewable-energy/#:~:text=The%20wind%2C%20the%20sun%2C%20and,we%20can%20see%20and%20feel.

Last accessed on 31/July/2020

Period 1

Introductory activity

Begin the class by discussing the question in **Reflect**. Show the students a few posters about environmental awareness. Ask the following leading questions to the students:

- What are natural resources and why are they important?
- What are the threats to the Earth's natural resources?
- What steps can be taken to conserve the natural resources?

Define natural resources and explain the two types of natural resources to the students.

Period 2

Define renewable resources and explain the importance of renewable resources such as air, water, soil, forests, wildlife, sunlight and wind. Ask the students to answer the question in **Figure Out**. Ask the students to complete the activity in **DIY**.

Period 3

Define non-renewable resources and explain the importance of non-renewable resources such as coal, petroleum, minerals and metals. Ask students to read out the fact in **FactPedia**. **Discuss** the question in **Think Box** and ask the students to write the answer in their notebooks. Ask the students to complete the **Picture Study**.

Period 4

Explain how overpopulation, land use and forests are a threat to the natural resources. Explain they ways in which natural resources can be conserved. Help the students answer the question in **Life Skills and Values.**

Period 5

Ask the students to read the points in **In a Nutshell**. Randomly ask a few students to explain each point and follow it with a discussion on the important points covered in the chapter.

Period 6

For a quick revision refer to **Snap Recap**. Ask students to answer the questions in **Workout**. Have them sit in pairs and ask them to discuss the answers.

Extended learning

Ask the students draw a terrestrial and an aquatic food web and make a comparison.

Role play: In groups, students can do a role play on Life Without Petroleum Products. They can discuss what might happen if the primary source of solar energy is absent.

Homework: Guide the students to make lemon squash and put them up for sale. The proceeds can be donated for charity.

18 Our Environment

Total required: 10 periods **Textbook Reference:** Page 120 to 125

Weblinks

For more information, visit

https://www.nationalgeographic.org/encyclopedia/autotroph/

https://climatekids.nasa.gov/climate-change-evidence/

Last accessed on 31/July/2020

Period 1

Introductory activity

Refer to **Reflect** and complete the given exercise. Initiate a discussion based on it. Ask the following questions to the students:

- Name three differences between living and non-living things.
- What are the components of the environment?
- Are the different components of environment interdependent?
- What is ecology?
- Why is it important to maintain a balance in nature?

Period 2

Read the chapter aloud till the topic 'Interdependence in Nature'. Discuss the components of the environment with the help of a **PowerPoint presentation**. Discuss the fact in **FactPedia**. Ask the students to answer the question in **Figure Out**.

Periods 3 and 4

Pull-out Booklet

Have the students fold a paper and divide it into four sections. In the first section, ask the students to write about biotic and abiotic factors. In the second section, the students can write a short comparison between the biotic and abiotic factors of the environment. Next they can make a pictorial depiction of the interdependence of the two factors. Finally, in the last section, students can draw and label how energy flows in the environment.

Period 5

Group work: Ask the students to explain the complete interdependence of the components of the environment. They can cut out pictures or draw and label appropriately.

Speaking activity: The students should be able to explain and answer questions based on it. Encourage the students to bring forth questions for the other groups.

Period 6

Extended learning

Show a few pictures related to globalization to the students and ask them to draw inferences about them. Ask leading questions about terms such as unity in diversity, interdependence and globalization. Taking a cue from this, ask the students what is meant by globalization. Encourage them to put forward their views. Read out the paragraphs on globalization and explain the impacts that it has on us and the environment. Encourage the students to talk about global warming.

Period 7

Ask the students to read aloud the points in **In a Nutshell**. Randomly ask some students to explain each point and then follow it with a discussion on the important points covered in the chapter. Explain and make them do **Think Box** and **Picture Study**.

Research: Homework: Find out the how multinational companies have impacted the economy of India. Refer to the **DIY**.

Period 8

Role-play: Follow the rubrics for **Life Skills and Values** and encourage the students to enact a short skit based on it.

Homework: Let the children complete **Enjoy** at home and read out their prescriptions in the class.

Period 9

For a quick revision refer to **Snap Recap**. Ask students answer the questions in **Workout**. Have them sit in pairs and ask them to discuss the answers.

Period 10

Pair work: Ask the students to discuss, plan and make effective posters. Later this can be displayed on the soft board.

19 Natural Disasters

Total required: 8 periods **Textbook Reference:** Page 126 to 134

Weblinks

For more information, visit

https://www.nationalgeographic.com/environment/natural-disasters/volcanoes/

https://www.natgeokids.com/au/discover/geography/physical-geography/tsunamis/

http://www.ndrf.gov.in/

Last accessed on 31/July/2020

Period 1

Introductory activity

A major news headline in the newspaper perturbed Humaira. She is a seismologist and predicts earthquakes so that disasters can be avoided.

News report

A strong earthquake of magnitude 7.8 Mw hit Nepal and adjoining regions on 25 April at 11:56 a.m. Nepal Standard Time. The earthquake has destroyed the infrastructure and reports of huge casualties have been coming in.

Humaira knew that South Asia is a seismically active zone. The tremors of this earthquake were felt in India too. Based on the given news, ask the students the following questions about natural disasters:

- Ask leading questions to students about disasters such as cloudbursts, volcanic eruptions, earthquakes, floods, droughts, tsunamis, hurricanes and landslides.
- What causes natural disasters?
- What is the aftermath of such disasters?
- What are the safety measures to be adopted when such natural disasters occur?

Ask the students to refer to **Reflect** and answer the questions. Read out the fact in **FactPedia**.

Period 2

Read the chapter aloud. Discuss the characteristics of different natural disasters. Ask the students to answer the question in **Figure Out** and do research work based on it.

Periods 3 and 4

Little Researchers: Enjoy

Divide the class into 5 groups. Let each group choose one of the natural disasters and work on the given rubrics. Provide wet potter's clay and ask students to make a model of a volcano. Place a big display tray where the students can arrange their models. Coloured powder paint or acrylic paint can be used to make it look realistic. Label the different parts.

Writing task: Ask students to write a short paragraph about the recent natural disaster they have read about.

Speaking activity: Ask the children to explain the phenomenon that takes place during such disasters.

Period 5

Extended learning

As a reinforcement, a worksheet with pictures or news headlines can be prepared for the children to work on.

After this activity, ask the students to read the points in **In a Nutshell**. Randomly ask some students to explain each point and then follow it with a discussion on the important points covered in the chapter.

Period 6

As mentioned in the **DIY** activity, have the students practise a mock evacuation drill. Discuss the important points to be remembered while facing any such disaster.

Period 7

Guide the students to do **Think Box** and **Picture Study**. Explain and make them do **Life Skills and Values** in class.

Period 8

For a quick revision refer to **Snap Recap**. Ask students to answer the questions in **Workout**. Have them sit in pairs and ask them to discuss the answers.

Worksheet

1. Evolution of Human Beings

Worksheet

A **Answer in one word.**

1. Early human beings who resembled apes: ....
2. Creatures that feed their young ones: ....
3. Early humans who hunted animals: ....
4. Remains of living things: ....

B **Correct the sentences.**

1. Early humans were called homo sapiens.

   ....

2. The hunter-gatherers ate fruits and roots of plants.

   ....

3. Hominids lived on the Earth only for a few years.

   ....

4. The remains of early humans were found in India.

   ....

C **How were the lives of early humans different from our lives?**

....

....

....

....

....

D **Name the different sources of information that helped historians to know about human evolution.**

....

....

....

....

....

....

Worksheet

A Match the following.

Column A	*Column B*
1. Palaeolithic Age	a. Copper Age
2. Chalcolithic Age	b. Beginning of agriculture
3. Mesolithic Age	c. Invention of wheel
4. Neolithic Age	d. Discovery of fire

B Write a short note on the pottery of the Neolithic Age.

....

....

....

C How did the domestication of animals help early humans?

....

....

....

D Draw three pictures describing the life of early humans. Write a sentence about each picture.

....

....

3. The Iron Age

Worksheet

A **Fill in the blanks with the correct answers.**

1. In the Chalcolithic Age, tools were made of .... (copper/iron).
2. Iron was first used in .... (east/west) Asia.
3. .... (Greek/Indus Valley) Civilization flourished in the Iron Age.
4. Trading of food grains began in the .... (Iron/Bronze) Age.

B **Explain in brief the factors that affected the life of people during the Iron Age.**

....

....

....

C **How did the discovery of bronze help early humans?**

....

....

....

D **What were the advantages of using iron over bronze in making tools?**

....

....

....

E **Draw and name three tools used during the Iron Age.**

Worksheet

A Fill in the blanks with the correct answers.

1. The steam engine was first designed by .... (James Watt/Thomas Newcomen).
2. The discovery of .... (coal/petroleum) lead to the 'birth of the modern automobile'.
3. Paper was invented by the .... (Chinese/Germans).
4. Many artificial satellites pick up signals from the Earth and then send them back through .... (internet/transmitters).

B Rewrite these sentences correctly.

1. Marco Polo travelled from Asia to Europe.

   ....

2. Video calls can be made using a fax machine.

   ....

3. Early humans used ink pens to write on clay tablets.

   ....

4. The first evidence of writing was found in Greece.

   ....

C Answer these questions.

1. Why is mass communication important? Name two means of mass communication.

   ....

   ....

   ....

2. Write a short note on two modern methods of communication

   ....

   ....

   ....

3. Write a short note on the invention of the steam engine.

   ....

   ....

   ....

5. The Indian Constitution

Worksheet

A Name the following.

1. The supreme law of India: ....
2. The head of the Constituent Assembly: ....
3. It is responsible for making the defence and foreign policy of India: ....
4. The introductory statement which explains the principles on which the Constitution of India was framed ....

B Write T for True and F for False.

1. The Constitution of India was first adopted on 26 January, 1950. ☐
2. The Constitution of India is the longest constitution in the world. ☐
3. 'Secular' means all Indians have an equal right to own a share of the country's wealth. ☐
4. 'Fraternity' means all Indians should live as a family. ☐

C Answer these questions.

1. Describe the nature of Constitution of India.

....

....

....

....

....

....

....

2. Why did India need a constitution after gaining independence from the British?

....

....

....

....

....

....

....

Worksheet

6. Fundamental Rights and Duties

Worksheet

A **Fill in the blanks.**

1. Human rights are based on principles of .... , ... and ....
2. .... is considered inhuman under the right to equality of the Indian Constitution.
3. The .... was added to the Constitution of India in 2009.
4. A .... is a public property.

B **Write R for rights and D for duties.**

1. Voting in the elections ☐
2. Keeping the environment clean ☐
3. Expressing an opinion ☐
4. Following one's religion ☐
5. Respecting people's privacy ☐

C **Answer these questions.**

1. Write any three fundamental duties of an Indian citizen.

....

....

....

....

....

2. How are the cultural and educational rights different from the right to education?

....

....

....

....

....

3. What are Human Rights?

....

....

....

....

....

7. The Indian Democracy

Worksheet

A Match the following.

Column A	*Column B*
1. Rajya Sabha	a. making laws for the state
2. Lok Sabha	b. foreign policy
3. Union List	c. lower house
4. State List	d. public health
5. State Legislature	e. upper house

B Rewrite these sentences correctly.

1. In a democracy no one has to follow any rules.

   ....

2. The union territories are governed by the state governments.

   ....

3. The high court is also known as 'sansad' in India.

   ....

4. The Speaker carries out the proceedings of the Rajya Sabha.

   ....

5. The members of the Rajya Sabha are elected directly by the people.

   ....

C Answer these questions.

1. Write a short note on the Indian judiciary.

   ....

   ....

   ....

2. Why are elections important?

   ....

   ....

   ....

3. How are the members of the Lok Sabha and Rajya Sabha elected?

   ....

   ....

   ....

8. Locating Places on the Earth

Worksheet

A **Label the important latitudes of the Earth.**

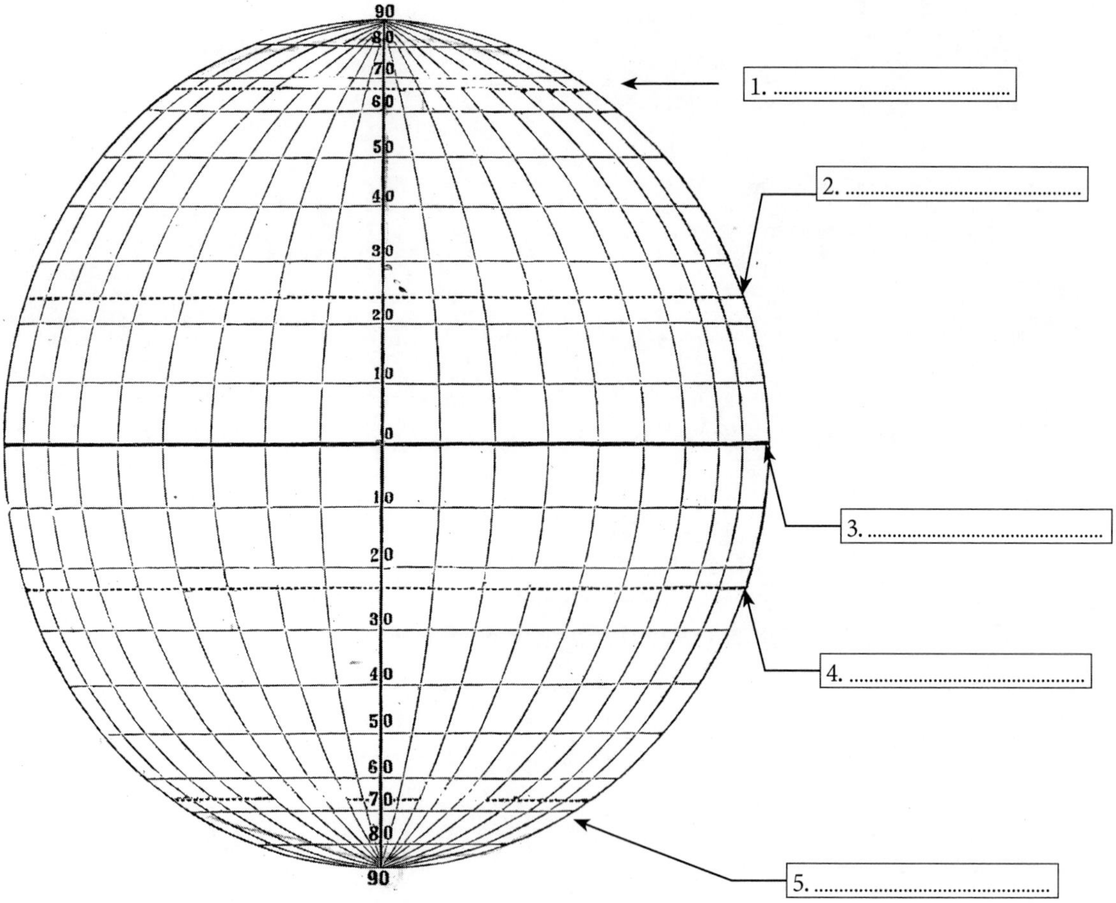

PARALLELS AND MERIDIANS

B **Rewrite these sentences correctly.**

1. The latitude measuring 66 ½ °N is known as the 'Great Circle'.

   ....

2. Longitudes are drawn from the east to the west.

   ....

3. The 0° longitude is known as the International Date Line.

   ....

4. Time is gained westwards of the International Date Line.

   ....

5. All latitudes are equal in length.

   ....

C **Answer these questions.**

1. Why are longitudes important?

....

....

....

....

....

....

2. Is the 20 °S latitude bigger than the 75 °S latitude? Elucidate your answer.

....

....

....

....

....

....

3. How are latitudes different from longitudes?

....

....

....

....

....

....

9. Weather and Climate

Worksheet

A Fill in the blanks.

1. The climate of the Earth is getting warmer because of ....
2. Weather data is collected based on the reading at a .... time.
3. Seasons change because of the Earth's .... around the Sun and the tilt of its ....
4. Some winds carry .... with them and cause rainfall.
5. .... is the amount of water vapour present in the atmosphere.

B Write the difference between:

1. Land breeze and sea breeze

....

....

....

2. Altitude and latitude

....

....

....

C Give reasons

1. Places near the poles are cold.

....

....

....

2. Places near the equator are hot.

....

....

....

D Answer these questions.

1. What is climate and how does it affect the lifestyle of people?

....

....

....

2. What is humidity ? How does it affect the climate of a place ?

....

....

....

10. The Major Temperature Zones

Worksheet

A Fill in the blanks with the correct answers.

1. The .... region is located between 10 °N and 10 °S of the Equator.
   a. equatorial   b. tropical
2. Albatross lives in the .... Hemisphere.
   a. Northern   b. Southern
3. The Masai tribe belongs to the ....
   a. tropical grassland regions   b. equatorial region
4. .... is located in the Frigid Zone
   a. Myanmar   b. Norway

B Rewrite these sentences correctly.

1. The climate changes frequently in places located near the Equator.

   ....

2. The tropical region is sparsely populated.

   ....

C Answer these questions.

1. Name the major climatic zones of the world.

   ....

   ....

2. Explain the difference between the climate of the Northern and the Southern Frigid zones.

   ....

   ....

D Give reasons

1. There is hardly any variation in the climate throughout the year in the Torrid Zone.

   ....

   ....

2. Equatorial regions are covered with rainforests.

   ....

   ....

3. The temperate grasslands are called by different names in different regions. Name them.

   ....

   ....

11. Eclipses

Worksheet

A **Fill in the blanks with the correct answers.**

1. During a lunar eclipse, the Earth blocks the .... from view.

   a. Moon b. Sun

2. When the Moon is completely blocked from view by the Earth, a .... lunar eclipse is said to have occurred.

   a. partial b. total

3. During a total lunar eclipse, the Moon appears ....

   a. dark b. brownish red

4. A lunar eclipse lasts for a few ....

   a. minutes b. hours

B **Give reasons.**

1. Special glasses should be worn while watching a solar eclipse.

   ....

2. It is safe to look at a lunar eclipse without wearing any glasses.

   ....

C **Answer these questions.**

1. How is a total solar eclipse different from a partial solar eclipse?

   ....

   ....

2. Why do we see the lunar eclipse only at night?

   ....

   ....

3. Regions that have high levels of air pollution cannot see the solar eclipse. Why?

   ....

   ....

D **Define these terms.**

1. eclipse

   ....

2. umbra

   ....

3. penumbra

   ....

12. India and Its Neighbours

Worksheet

A Match the countries to their capitals.

Column A	*Column B*
1. Nepal	a. Islamabad
2. China	b. Thimpu
3. Pakistan	c. Naypyidaw
4. Bhutan	d. Beijing
5. Bangladesh	e. Kathmandu
6. Myanmar	f. Dhaka

B Fill in the blanks with the correct answers.

1. India is the .... largest country in Asia.
   a. second b. third c. seventh
2. The Gobi Desert is located in ....
   a. Pakistan b. China c. Myanmar
3. The administrative capital of Sri Lanka is .
   a. Sri Jayawardenepura Kotte b. Colombo c. Jaffna
4. Bhutan is located in the .... Himalayas.
   a. northern b. western c. eastern

C On an outline political map of India, mark the following:

Delhi, all the neighbouring countries, water bodies

Worksheet

13. Climate of India

Worksheet

A Name the following.

1. The thunderstorm that bring relief to the eastern coastal regions in summer months: ....
2. Hot and dry wind that blows in North India during summer: ....
3. The state that receives the heaviest rainfall in India: ....
4. That state that receives the lowest rainfall in India: ....

B Write T for True and F for False.

1. Every region of India experiences only three seasons. ☐
2. The Thar Desert does not experience winter. ☐
3. Tamil Nadu receives heavy rainfall in winter. ☐
4. Winter is followed by the autumn season. ☐

C Answer these questions.

1. List the factors that affect the climate of a place.

....

....

....

....

2. Explain the weather conditions of the tropical and semi-arid climate. Name the regions of India that experience these types of climate.

....

....

....

....

3. Explain why the coastal regions of India don't have a severe winter.

....

....

....

....

4. Name the different types of climates of India.

....

....

....

....

14. Natural Vegetation of India

Worksheet

A Match the following.

Column A	*Column B*
1. Tropical evergreen forest	a. grass
2. Deciduous or monsoon type forests	b. datepalm
3. Dry deciduous forests	c. Sundari
4. Semi-desert and desert vegetation	d. ebony
5. Tidal forests	e. fir
6. Mountain forests	f. rosewood

B Fill in the blanks.

1. The trees in .... forest stay green throughout the year.
2. The mountain vegetation varies according to .... , ... and ....
3. Forests prevent .... in hilly regions.
4. .... is a tree planting festival in India.

C Answer these questions in brief.

1. What are the special characteristics of trees found in tidal forests.

....

....

....

2. Where are the deciduous forests found in India?

....

....

....

3. Why should we conserve forests?

....

....

....

4. Why is there no vegetation on the highest mountain peaks?

....

....

....

5. What is Social Forestry?

....

....

....

15. Agriculture

Worksheet

A Answer in one word.

1. A beverage made from berries: ....
2. Animal waste that can be used as a fertilizer: ....
3. A plant that grows best in coastal regions: ....
4. A fruit farm: ....
5. A juice that makes food sweet: ....

B Identify the kharif and rabi crops.

1. Sugarcane ....
2. Wheat ....
3. Pulses ....
4. Bajra ....
5. Maize ....

C Answer these questions.

1. What are orchards and what type of crops are grown in orchards?

....

....

....

2. Write a short note on livestock rearing in India.

....

....

....

3. Why are millets a suitable crop for the drier regions?

....

....

....

4. What is the Green Revolution?

....

....

....

Worksheet

16. Industries

Worksheet

A Fill in the blanks with the correct answers.

1. A .... is a large scale industry.
   a. hosiery b. chemicals c. handmade paper
2. Small scale industries require ....
   a. lot of skilled labour b. locally produced raw materials c. a lot of capital
3. .... is a cottage industry .
   a. hand spun khadi b. jute industry c. petroleum
4. The information technology industry is a .... industry.
   a. large scale b. small scale c. cottage industry

B Fill in the blanks.

1. Large scale industries are very big ....
2. .... is a kind of natural fuel.
3. A good .... is required to transport the manufactured product to different regions.
4. Modern .... is used for producing goods in large scale industries.
5. The Central Pollution Control Board (CPCB) was set up to control ....
6. .... helps to promote economic growth of a country.

C Answer these questions.

1. What is industrialization?

   ....

   ....

   ....

2. How does industrial development help the economy of a country?

   ....

   ....

   ....

3. How does the government help the cottage industries?

   ....

   ....

   ....

4. Why are large scale industries located in the areas where raw material is available easily?

   ....

   ....

   ....

17. Natural Resources

Worksheet

A Answer these questions.

1. How do fossil fuels form?

....

....

....

2. Name four renewable resources.

....

....

....

B Fill in the blanks.

1. Ocean water is used for making .... and .... , ...
2. Only .... of the Earth's water is fresh.
3. .... resources are derived from plants, fossils and animals.
4. The .... converts the Sun's energy into ....
5. States such as .... and .... produce wind energy.
6. Petroleum is processed in a ....

C Give reasons

1. Soil is an important natural resource.

....

....

....

2. CNG is a cleaner fuel.

....

....

....

3. Land overuse is a threat to our natural resources.

....

....

....

Worksheet

Worksheet

A Match the columns.

Column A	*Column B*
1. acid rain	a. layer of the Earth where life exists.
2. ozone layer	b. global warming
3. polar ice caps	c. protective layer of atmosphere
4. unseasonal rain	d. Arctic/Antarctic regions
5. biosphere	e. damages crops

B Answer these questions.

1. What is the impact of local events on environment?

....

....

....

....

2. What are effects of global warming?

....

....

....

....

3. Autotrophs and heterotrophs are both necessary for life to exist. Why?

....

....

....

....

4. Do you think interdependence in the environment is necessary? Give reasons to support your answer.

....

....

....

....

Worksheet

A **Match the columns.**

Column A	*Column B*
1. drought	a. extinct volcano
2. famine	b. fast rotating winds
3. hurricane	c. tidal wave
4. tsunami	d. dormant volcano
5. Mauna Loa	e. seismograph
6. Mount Popa	f. lava
7. magma	g. acute shortage of food
8. earthquake	h. long spells of no rainfall

B **Write a short note on seismology.**

....

....

....

....

C **How do forest fires occur?**

....

....

....

....

D **How does a natural disaster affect our lives?**

....

....

....

....

E **Explain how drought affect farmers and the population of a country?**

....

....

....

....

Answer Keys

1. Evolution of Human Beings

Reflect

*Climatic change, volcanic eruption, Ice Age

Figure Out

Thumbs

Workout

A 1. F 2. T 3. T 4. F

B 1. extinct 2. hominids 3. Africa 4. homo sapiens

C
1. Two million years ago, humans resembled apes and were called hominids.
2. Early humans used their hands to hold objects.
3. The early humans wore animal skin and used leaves to cover themselves.
4. The early humans moved from place to place in search of food.

D
1. Slowly , the hominids began to change and after many years, they developed features that we see in humans today. For instance, they could stand upright and gained the ability to hold objects.
2. The ability to balance on their feet helped them to stand and walk erect, thereby making their hands free. They could now use their hands to make tools, pick up and throw things.
3. The hunter-gatherers did not stay in one place. They led a simple life, moving from place to place, hunting animals and eating fruits and roots and catching fish. When they ran out of food in one place, they moved to a new place. They lived in caves or on tree tops to protect themselves from wild animals. They wore animal skin and used leaves to cover themselves.
4. We get information about early humans mainly from caves and rock shelters, skeletal remains or bones of early humans, tools that they used, artefacts, fossils and bones and horns of animals. These are our sources of information.

Think Box

Answers will vary

Picture Study

1. hunting 2. cave dwellers
3. The Ajanta and the Ellora caves

Life Skills and Values

In order to protect themselves from the harsh climate, early humans started living in caves. They used animal skin to cover themselves in order to avoid cold weather. Now, people have different means to adapt to their environment, such as, heavy clothing, gadgets like an air conditioner, heaters etc.

Enjoy

Let's Go Fishing

2. The Stone Age

Reflect

*I can use a stone to play a game, I can use a stone as a paper weight and I can use stones to decorate my plant holder.

Figure Out

Microliths are small and sharp tools that were used by the early humans, especially, during the Stone Age.

Workout

A 1. F 2. F 3. F 4. T

B 1. cooked food 2. Copper 3. dog 4. flint

C
1. The three periods of the Stone Age are the Palaeolithic Age or the Old Stone Age, the Mesolithic Age or the Middle Stone Age and the Neolithic Age or the New Stone Age.
2. While making stone tools, early humans discovered that fire could be produced by rubbing two dry stones together.
3. In the Neolithic Age, stone sickles were used for harvesting crops and axes with wooden handles were used for cutting trees. Early humans also made a digging stick for tilling soil.
4. During the Chalcolithic Age, early humans started using tools made of copper along with stone tools. However, in the Stone Age, they used only stone tools.

D
1. During the Palaeolithic Age, humans were mainly hunter gatherers. They moved from place to place in search of food. They lived in caves and covered themselves with leaves and animal skin. They ate wild berries, roots, meat and fish. The tools they used, were made of stones, wood or bones. These tools were crude and had sharp edges. Early humans learnt how to sharpen a stone with another stone. Hand axes with sharp edges belonging to this age have been discovered. It was during this period that early humans began to communicate with each other and the first form of language developed.
2. The invention of the wheel brought about a change in the life of early humans as they could now travel easily from one place to another using carts that had wheels.

***Please note:** The answers with * are sample which may vary*

They could also carry heavy loads on these carts. The potter's wheel was invented and used by humans much later. They used it for making pots to store grains.

3. The tools used in the Palaeolithic Age were made of stones, wood or bones. These tools were crude and had sharp edges. However, in the Neolithic Age as humans began farming, better tools were needed for sowing seeds, tilling soil and harvesting crops. Although made from stone still, polished tools were used in place of crude stone tools. Early humans started chiseling stone tools to make them sharper. Stone sickles were used for harvesting crops and axes with wooden handles were used for cutting trees. Early humans also made a digging stick for tilling soil. They used bones to make needles and spindles.
4. The Neolithic, or the New Stone Age, saw a lot of advancement in human evolution. Early humans began to understand the importance of farming and were moving towards a more settled life. As early humans started farming, better tools were needed for sowing seeds, tilling soil and harvesting crops. They started chiseling stone tools to make them sharper. Stone sickles were used for harvesting crops and axes with wooden handles were used for cutting trees. Early humans also made a digging stick for tilling soil.

Think Box

Grinding stone, quartz watch

Picture Study

A The Palaeolithic Age

B During this time, humans were mainly hunter-gatherers. They moved from place to place in search of food. They lived in caves and covered themselves with leaves and animal skin. They ate wild berries, roots, meat and fish. The tools they used, were made of stones, wood or bones.

Life Skills and Values

As humans developed the concept of farming, they did not feel the need to travel from place to place in search of food. Thus they felt the need to settle down in one place. As early humans started leading settled lives, the concept of family evolved. People now divided their responsibilities and work. Not everybody had to do the same work. This led to the dependency on different members and led to the concept of living in groups also for safety.

Across the Boundary I

Down: telegram, rock paintings made by early humans, an ancient seal, a stamp, Sun Temple, Konark; a fossil, ruins of Nalanda, Ashoka Pillar in Sarnath

3. The Iron Age

Reflect

silver, iron, copper, gold

Figure Out

The Indus Valley Civilization, 3000 BCE; River Indus The Mesopotamian Civilization, 5000–3500 BCE, Rivers Tigris and Euphrates

Figure Out

Smelting is the process of removing pure metal from its ore by melting it at very high temperatures.

Figure Out

The Greek and the Roman civilizations flourished during the Iron Age.

Workout

A 1. T 2. F 3. F 4. F

B 1. trade 2. cheap, available 3. bronze 4. ores

C 1. plough 2. ironaxe 3. sickle 4. sword

D

1. Better tools improved farming techniques. This led to an increased agricultural output and production of surplus grains. With enough grains in store, early humans started trade. The beginning of trade led to the rise of cities.
2. Iron was used widely as it was available easily during the Iron Age. Farmers could use an iron axe, making it easy to plough land or break stones. Iron was also used for making sickles for harvesting crops and ploughshares for turning and digging the soil.
3. An increase in the demand for cultivable land led to conflicts among people that ultimately caused wars. The use of iron also led to an increase in weapon production. Weapons such as swords, spears and arrowheads were made. Tribes with iron weapons had an advantage over tribes that did not have iron weapons. There were constant fights amongst people and a powerful ruler was needed to bring in peace.
4. Selling and buying of food grains started in towns and villages during the Iron Age. Trade relationships were established with distant regions. To carry out trade, money was needed. Hence, coins were made with iron.

E

1. Using iron to make tools had many advantages. Iron was cheap and easily available. It was strong and sturdy and ideal for making agricultural implements. Iron was a better metal than bronze as bronze had to be made by mixing copper and tin, which was not easily available. Iron could be easily extracted from its ore. Besides, bronze was softer than iron.
2. An increase in the demand for cultivable land led to conflicts among people that ultimately caused wars. The use of iron also led to an increase in weapon production. Weapons such as swords, spears and arrowheads were made. Tribes with iron weapons had an advantage over tribes that did not have iron weapons. There were constant fights amongst

people and a powerful ruler was needed to bring in peace. Thus, the concept of kingship evolved.

3. The discovery of iron was a turning point in the history of the world. Using iron to make tools had many advantages. It was strong and sturdy and ideal for making agricultural implements. Farmers could use an iron axe, making it easy to plough the land or to break stones. Iron was also used for making sickles for harvesting crops and ploughshares for turning and digging the soil. To carry out trade, money was needed. Hence, coins were made with iron. During the Iron Age, vehicles, boats and ships were manufactured. This improved the transport system and trade with distant lands grew.
4. People in the Iron Age started practising new occupations such as construction, crafts and pottery. Nails and rivets were made by ironsmiths. Some people were traders who traded with distant lands.

Think Box

During the Iron Age, early humans discovered that a high temperature coal fire could be used for the extraction of iron from iron ores.

Picture Study

1. Iron
2. Farmers could use an iron axe, making it easy to plough the land or to break stones. Iron was also used for making sickles for harvesting crops and ploughshares for turning and digging the soil.

4. Evolution of Transport and Communication

Reflect

1. *In a carriage or on a horseback
2. *I go to school in a school bus.
3. We now have advanced and much faster moving vehicles.

Figure Out

Pressure cooker

Figure Out

Papyrus is a plant that grows wild all over the Nile river valley, it was used for writing with ink.

DIY

1. I see a stamped envelope in the picture.
2. This is an individual communication.
3. It helps us to communicate with people who live faraway.

Workout

A 1. Vasco da Gama 2. Wilbur and Orville Wright 3. Ferdinand Magellan 4. Hieroglyphics

B 1. b 2. c 3. e 4. a 5. d

C 1. ideas, information 2. clay tablets 3. steam engine 4. printing press 5. computer, internet

D

1. Ferdinand Magellan sailed westwards to explore East Indies. He was the first explorer to complete a circumnavigation of the Earth, proving that the Earth is round.
2. In earlier days, homing pigeons or carrier pigeons were trained to carry messages to distant places. Messages would be written on small pieces of paper and tied to the pigeon's feet. These pigeons had the natural ability to find their way home with a return message.
3. In 1440, Johannes Gutenberg, invented the printing press. This was one of the most important discoveries made in the field of communication. He used moveable metal or wooden letters to form words and sentences. Ink was applied on moulds of alphabets and sheets of paper were printed. The moulds could be reset and reused.
4. *Motor bikes, jet plane, metro rail, auto rickshaw

E

1. A great revolution in the field of transportation was the invention of the steam engine. The first train pulled by a steam engine was made approximately 200 years ago. Around the same time, ships running on steam engines were also used. Thus, travelling became easier and faster and heavy goods could be transported easily.
2. Personal communication means sharing of information between two individuals. Mass communication is used for communicating information to large a number of people at a time.
3. Telegraph helps in sending messages quickly using an electrical connection. Telephone is an instrument using which people can talk to one another. Typewriter is a machine that leaves an impression of letters on paper when the user presses a key. It is used to type letters, notes, and books. Radio is a machine through which information or a message can be transmitted in the form of sound waves. Television is a means of mass communication used for delivering information and for entertainment in the form of visuals.
4. Many artificial satellites are sent into the Earth's orbit. They pick up signals from the Earth and then send them back through transmitters. It is because of these satellites that we get to see what is happening in the other parts of the world instantly, or watch live telecasts of cricket and football matches sitting at home. Satellites also help meteorologists forecast weather or climate.

Think Box

Some mobile phones are called smart phones as they can do more than other phones. They work as a computer but are mobile devices small enough to fit in a user's hand.

Picture Study

1. An artificial satellite   2. Earth's orbit.
3. They pick up signals from the Earth and then send them back through transmitters. It is because of these satellites that we get to see what is happening in the other parts of the world instantly, or watch live telecasts of cricket and football matches sitting at home. Satellites also help meteorologists forecast weather or climate.

Life Skills and Values

A 1. We can communicate with a friend who lives in a different continent through, telephone, emails, smartphones.

2. Animals communicate with each other by making sounds.

B ISD stands for International Subscriber Dialing. It involves making an international telephone call that is dialed directly by a telephone subscriber, rather than by a telephone operator. STD stands for Subscriber Trunk Dialing. It is a telephone system that allows subscribers to make trunk calls or make calls outside the state without operator assistance.

Across the Boundary 2

A map showing the route taken by Magellan and the coasts discovered by him.

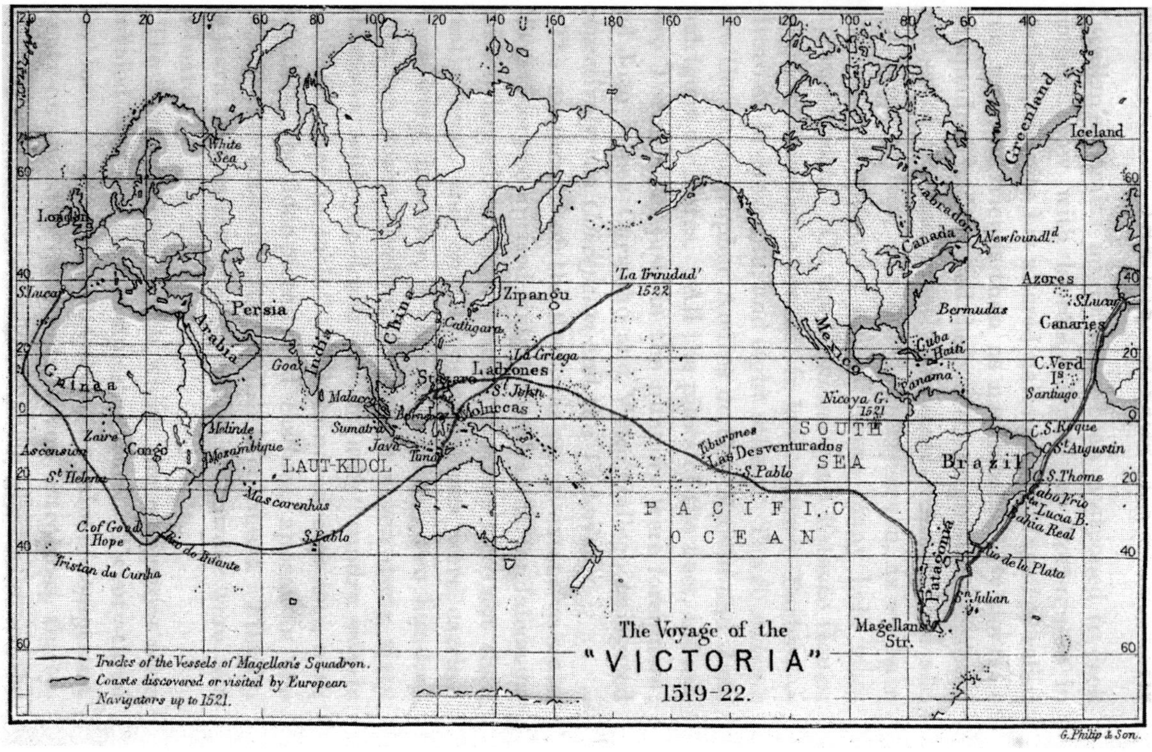

5. The Indian Constitution

Reflect

*A government gets its power from the people of a country who have voted to elect them.

Figure Out

The Constitution Day, also known as Samvidhan Divas, is celebrated in India on 26 November every year to commemorate the adoption of the Constitution of India. On this day in 1949, the Constituent Assembly of India adopted the Constitution of India, and it came into effect on 26 January 1950.

Workout

A 1. The Constituent Assembly
2. supreme   3. Preamble
4. equality, justice and liberty.

B 1. c   2. b   3. a

C 1. sovereign   2. fraternity   3. liberty   4. equality

D 1. The main task of the Constituent Assembly was to frame the Constitution.
2. In India, the system of government is parliamentary democracy.
3. The preamble says 'justice' means all citizens, irrespective of their background, should be treated fairly, honestly and equally and have the right to vote in the elections.
4. Liberty means the freedom to speak and write what one thinks, freedom to choose one's religion, freedom to travel anywhere, and freedom to live in one's place of choice.

E 1. All republics like India have a set of rules or principles that have to be followed by every citizen. These rules also help in governing the country. When India attained freedom, it was facing many socio-economic issues. Many people were uneducated and they were divided by the caste system. Equality among the people could be achieved only by making it a law so that everybody would get the same opportunities

2. The Constitution of India begins with a Preamble, which is an introductory statement that explains the principles on which the Constitution of India is based.
3. The laws written in our Constitution are based on the values of justice, equality, liberty and fraternity. 'Justice' means all citizens, irrespective of their background, should be treated fairly, honestly and equally and have the right to vote in the elections. 'Liberty' means the freedom to speak and write what one thinks, freedom to choose one's religion, freedom to travel anywhere, and freedom to live in one's place. 'Equality' means every Indian citizen has a right to equal opportunities irrespective of their religion, economic status, sex or place of birth. 'Fraternity' means all Indians should live as a family and consider each other as brothers and sisters despite differences.
4. 'Secular' means equal freedom and respect for all the religions. People could follow any religion of their choice and practise religious rituals freely.

Think Box

A The original copies of the Constitution were written in both English and Hindi so that it could be understood by people who speak these languages. India has a considerably large number of Hindi and English speaking people.

Picture Study

1. The building is Parliament House or Sansad Bhavan.
2. New Delhi
3. The Parliament House or Sansad Bhavan is where our elected parliamentarians sit and discuss a number of important issues related to national interest.

6. Fundamental Rights and Duties

Reflect

Answers will vary

Figure Out

The Midday Meal Scheme is an initiative of the Government of India. Under this scheme, free meals are provided, on working days, to children studying in government and government-aided institutions. It was introduced in order to improve the nutritional status of the children in India.

DIY

A

Column 1 Down:	Duty	Right	Duty
Column 2 Down:	Right	Duty	Right

Workout

A 1. R 2. D 3. R 4. R 5. R 6. D

B 1 d 2. a 3. e 4. f 5. c 6. b

C

1. A right is a freedom that is protected. A duty is a responsibility that people have towards their family, school, home, community or country.
2. Our rights are based on principles of equality, respect and justice.
3. The six fundamental rights that our constitution has given us are right to equality, right to freedom, right to freedom of religion, right against exploitation, cultural and educational rights, right to constitutional remedies
4. Right to education entitles every child in the age group of 5 to 14 the right to free basic education.

D

1. Right to freedom of religion:

   It the right to choose and follow any religion. Everyone has the freedom to follow their religious beliefs. People have the freedom to manage their own religious affairs.

   Right to equality:

   The right to equality states that all people are equal before the law. People cannot be discriminated on grounds of religion, race, caste, gender or place of birth. Equality of opportunity in employment is also a part of the right to equality. Untouchability is considered inhuman under the right to equality.
2. Cultural rights grant the people the freedom to promote and nurture their culture. Educational rights ensure that all students can get admission in any educational institution irrespective of their caste, religion, race or language.
3. The right against exploitation prohibits the employment of children below 14 years of age. However, the right to education entitles every child in the age group of 5 to 14 the right to free basic education
4. The fundamental duties for all the citizens of India are:
   - To obey the laws in the Constitution and follow them
   - To respect the National Flag and the National Anthem
   - To protect the unity and honour of India
   - To defend the country and offer our service when it is required to encourage peace and harmony among all the people of India and treat them like brothers and sisters
   - To guard our environment and look after forests, rivers and wildlife
   - To protect all public property such as monuments and historical sites

Think Box

In the first picture we see children going to school but in the second picture children are working instead of attending school. The second picture violates the fundamental right–the right against exploitation which prohibits the employment of children below 14 years of age. It also violates the right to education–which entitles every child in the age group of 5 to 14 the right to free basic education.

Picture Study

1. Right to freedom
2. Ans will vary

7. The Indian Democracy

Reflect

*No, it should not as India is a democracy where every citizen is considered to be equal.

Figure Out

Apart from India, USA, Sweden, Iceland have democratic governments.

Figure Out

A coalition government is a government in which several parties cooperate to run the country.

Figure Out

The Lok Sabha consists of 552 members

DIY

*Answers will vary

Workout

A
1. union list
2. executive
3. constituencies
4. speaker

B
1. the legislature, the executive and the judiciary
2. concurrent list
3. opposition
4. State Legislature
5. Supreme Court

C
1. The distribution of power between the state and the central governments is done in three lists—the union list, the state list and the concurrent list.
2. A political party is a group of people who have same political beliefs.
3. The president, the vice president, the prime minister and the cabinet ministers, are all members of the executive.
4. Citizens of India, who are above 18 years of age, are eligible to vote in general election to elect the members of the Lok Sabha. Citizens should vote so as to choose their leaders, who are answerable to them. If the voters are unsatisfied with the performance of a leader, they can vote them out in the next election.

D
1. The main function of the legislature is to make laws. The executive implements the laws passed by the legislature. The main function of the judiciary is to settle disputes according to the laws and ensure that justice is delivered. It also ensures that the rights of all Indian citizens are protected.
2. Any citizen who is above 25 years of age is allowed to contest elections for the Lok Sabha. Many political parties take part in an election. Every political party selects one member to contest the election from its constituency. The political parties organize campaigns to explain to the people the changes or developments that will be carried out, should they vote for their party. The candidate who gets the maximum number of votes, wins the election.
3. As a responsible citizen of India, it is our duty to vote wisely and elect the right leader. We should not resort to unfair means of voting. While electing our leaders, we should not be influenced by anyone and vote justly. We should take into consideration the rights of others while exercising our own rights and duties. We should respect and obey laws of the land and be tolerant to the religious beliefs of others. It is our responsibility to take care of public property and our heritage and take measures to save the environment.

Think Box

A It is important to have an opposition as they act as a check on the policies of the government.

B 1, 3 and 4

Picture Study

Press conference in a democracy is important as it helps the leaders to explain directly the reasons behind their policies and deeds making it transparent to the public.

8. Locating Places on the Earth

Reflect

library: E, 1

police station: D, 4

post office: D, 2

school: A, 3

Figure Out

Greenwich Mean Time

DIY

1. South America, Africa, Asia
2. Madagascar
3. 8°44' to 37°6' north latitude and 68°7' to 97°25' east longitude
4. Australia

Workout

A
1. Longitudes
2. 23 °N
3. Antarctic Circle
4. Prime Meridian

B 1. d 2. c 3. e 4. b 5. a

C
1. Latitudes are imaginary lines that are drawn from east to west. These latitudes run parallel to each other. Imaginary lines that are drawn from north to south are called longitudes. They meet at the poles.
2. Latitudes and longitudes form grid or network of lines meeting at intersections. The grid helps to locate places.
3. The International Date Line is the 180 degrees longitude opposite to Prime Meridian.
4. The Equator is called the Great Circle.

D Refer to diagram on pg 55 of the book

E
1. Properties of latitudes
   - Latitudes extend from the east to the west.
   - They run parallel to one another.
   - Latitudes vary in size, they are longer near the Equator and shortest near the poles.
   - There are 181 latitudes.
2. Properties of longitudes
   - Longitudes extend from the North Pole to the South Pole.
   - Prime Meridian or 0° longitude passes through Greenwich in England.
   - The distance between the longitudes is the widest at the Equator, gradually the gap between them reduces till they meet at the poles.
   - All longitudes are equal in length.
   - Longitudes help us figure out the time of a place.
3. The Earth takes about 24 hours or 1440 minutes to complete one rotation. Therefore, it takes 1440 ÷ 360, that is, 4 minutes to move one degree. This means the time difference between two meridians is 4 minutes.

Think Box

They travelled westwards. We lose time as sun rises later. We calculate 4 minutes for every longitude.

Picture Study

1. Africa 2. Equator 3. Uganda/ Congo/Kenya

Life Skills and Values

Yes, the latitude and longitude will help us to know our exact location.

Across the Boundary 3

Delhi: 28.7041° N, 77.1025° E

Gujarat: 22.2587° N, 71.1924° E

Kerala: 10.8505° N, 76.2711° E

West Bengal: 22.9868° N, 87.8550° E

9. Weather and Climate

Reflect

1. Tuesday
2. Monday
3. Monday and Wednesday
4. An umbrella
5. Cloudy

Figure Out

Antarctica

Workout

A 1. season 2. weather 3. latitudes 4. altitude

B 1. T 2. F 3. F 4. F

C 1. foggy 2. humid 3. breezy 4. cloudy

D
1. Spring, summer, autumn, monsoon, winter.
2. Weather is the condition of the atmosphere at a particular place over a short period of time, like, day to day or from week to week.
3. Climate is the average condition of a place over a long period of time.
4. The altitude, distance from the sea, the latitude, winds and humidity.

E
1. Weather is the condition of the atmosphere at a particular place over a short period of time. The climate of a place is the average weather condition of a place over a long period of time.
2. During daytime, the land heats up faster than the sea and makes the air column above it warm. This warm air rises, creating a vacuum which is filled in by the cool air from the sea. This is known as the sea breeze. During night, the opposite happens. The water gets heated up faster than land. The air above the water rises and the cool air from the land fills up the place. This is known as land breeze. (Refer to the diagram on page 64)
3. Wind also affects the climate of a place. Winds originating from the hills are cooler than the winds originating from the desert. Some winds carry moisture in them and cause rainfall.
4. Places near the Equator receive direct rays of the Sun. Places near the poles receive slating rays of the Sun. As the rays have to travel for a longer distance, they lose their heat. Hence, we can say that the places near the Equator are hotter than the places located near the poles.

Think Box

- It's getting hotter.
- Change in weather pattern.
- Tornadoes, hurricanes have increased.
- Torrential rain leading to flooding in some areas, no rain in other areas.

Picture Study

1. sunny 2. partly sunny 3. cloudy
4. lightning 5. heavy rain 6. slight showers

10. The Major Temperature Zones

Reflect

1. latitude 2. distance from the sea
3. winds 4. altitude
5. factors that affect climate

Figure Out

A person who studies climate is called a climatologist.

Workout

A 1. Equator 2. Savannah 3. hot deserts 4. Prairies

B 1. T 2. F 3. T 4. T 5. T

C **Torrid:** Myanmar, Malaysia, India, North Australia, Nigeria

Temperate: Alaska, New Zealand, Europe North Asia, United Kingdom, South Africa South Australia, Central America

Frigid: Antarctica, Greenland, Alaska, North Canada

D
1. The Earth is divided into three climatic or temperature zones according to their latitudinal location and prevailing climate.
2. The Sun's rays fall directly over the Torrid Zone area so there is hardly any variation in temperature throughout the year.
3. Frigid Zone
4. Antarctica

E
1. The Tropical grassland experiences a humid, hot and rainy summer and a cool and dry winter. The vegetation includes tall grass and acacia, and the wildlife comprises a variety of animals like zebras, giraffes, deer, rhinoceros, lions and leopards.
2. The Torrid Zone lies between the Equator and the Tropic of Cancer (23 ½° N) in the Northern Hemisphere and between the Equator and the Tropic of Capricorn (23 ½° S) in the Southern Hemisphere.
3. The countries that are in Europe, North Asia, Central America, Sothern Australia, Southern America and Southern Africa fall in the Temperate Zone. The Sun never shines directly overhead in this region and hence the climate is milder with temperatures ranging from warm to cool.
4. Northern Frigid Zone: Extremely cold, mostly frozen, blizzards in winter, in summer small regions have melted snow, moss, lichen and small berry plants grow here, sparsely populated.

   Southern Frigid Zone: Frozen throughout the year, extremely cold and windy, no vegetation, no population, only tourists, researchers and scientists.

Think Box

Norway is called 'the land of the midnight Sun' because in the summer months the sun does not set till midnight.

Picture Study

1. Antarctica
2. They are the coldest regions of the Earth and are covered with ice and snow.

11. Eclipses

Reflect

1. rotation 2. revolution

Figure Out

Once in 18 months, visible from some places on the Earth.

Workout

A
1. straight
2. solar, lunar
3. umbra, penumbra
4. minutes

B 1. solar 2. umbra 3. total 4. at night

C 1. T 2. F 3. T 4. T

D
1. An eclipse occurs when one celestial object blocks another celestial object from view.
2. During a lunar eclipse, the Earth, while revolving around the Sun, comes between the Sun and the moon.
3. During an eclipse the umbra is the darkest part of the shadow of the Moon. Penumbra is the outer area of the shadow.

E
1. A solar eclipse occurs when the Moon comes in between the Sun and the Earth causing a shadow to fall on certain parts of the Earth. A lunar eclipse occurs when the Earth, while revolving in its orbit around the Sun, comes in between the Sun and the Moon and prevents the Sun's rays from falling on the Moon. Solar eclipse happens during the day while lunar eclipse happens at night.
2. For diagram, refer to page 75
3. The Moon does not have its own light so it is safe to look at a lunar eclipse at night. During a solar eclipse the harmful rays of the sun may damage our eyes if we look directly at the sun. We should use special sun glasses.
4. For diagram, refer to page 76

Think Box

Most animals and birds react to a solar eclipse much like they do to nighttime. For example, bees and ants return to their nests and daytime birds return to their roosts in preparation to sleep; nighttime birds become noisy and active; bats start flying and hunting; mosquitoes start biting; and dairy cattle stop grazing, since they prefer to eat during daylight.

Picture Study

1. Lunar Eclipse

2. This happens when the Earth comes between the sun and the Moon.

Enjoy

eclipse, solar, partial, total, penumbra, umbra, lunar, shadow

12. India and Its Neighbours

Reflect

1. Asia
2. The Arabian Sea, the Bay of Bengal, the Indian Ocean
3. Myanmar, Bangladesh

Figure Out

It is a very large landmass which has all the different kinds of physical features and a variety of water bodies.

Figure Out

The Silk Route is the land route that travellers and traders took from Rome to China. It is called so because they traded in silk and other goods.

DIY

1. east 2. Bay of Bengal

Workout

A 1. T 2. T 3. F 4. T

B 1. c 2. e 3. b 4. a 5. d

C
1. Palk Strait
2. Kabul
3. Nepal
4. Ganga, Brahmaputra and Meghna

D
1. The Himalayan Mountain Range forms the natural boundary between India and China in the northern and the northeastern parts of India. Hiuen Tsang and Fa-Hien were two famous Chinese monks, who travelled to India and wrote travelogues about India. Historically, India and China had strong trade links with each other through the Silk Route.
2. The Indian subcontinent is located in Asia which is the largest continent of the Earth. India extends from 8 °N to 37 °N latitude, and 68 °E to 98 °E longitude.
3. Bhutan lies in the eastern Himalayas. It is a country surrounded by hills. Bhutan shares boundaries with West Bengal and Assam to the south, with Arunachal Pradesh to east, and with Sikkim to the southwest. Bhutan is divided into three physical regions—the Greater Himalayas, the Lesser Himalayas and the Dooars Plains. Torsa, Wong, Sankosh and Manas are the major rivers of Bhutan. Thimpu is the capital of Bhutan.
4. Myanmar was formerly called Burma. Burma was a part of India under the British rule. The Irrawaddy river has a rich fertile delta region where crops are cultivated. Ruby, a precious stone from Myanmar, is used for making jewellery. India and Myanmar share a geographical border in the northeastern part of India. The region is forested. A new highway India–Myanmar–Thailand (IMT) trilateral highway, is being built between India, Myanmar and Thailand to connect all three countries. The capital of Myanmar is Naypyidaw.

Think Box

The SAARC secretariat is located in Kathmandu. It is an economic and geopolitical organization of 8 Asian countries–India, Pakistan, Bangladesh, Nepal, Bhutan, Maldives, Afghanistan and Sri Lanka. It was formed to exhilarate economic growth and cultural development in South Asia. The member countries aim to strengthen cooperation among themselves at international forums on matters of common interest. Understanding each other's problems and collaboration in the field of economics, culture and technology and science are part of their programme.

(extra information on the countries is to be gathered by the students)

Picture Study

1. Great Wall of China 2. China 3. northern

13. Climate of India

Reflect

1. 28 January, 1885 2. 18.1 °C 3. 2.1 °C

Figure Out

The higher we go, the colder it gets. Hence, temperature decreases when altitude increases.

Figure Out

Ladakh is snow bound with hardly any vegetation.

DIY

1. October 2. July, August
3. March 4. December 5. City A

Workout

A
1. location
2. five
3. December, January, February
4. monsoon

B 1. d 2. c 3. b 4. e 5. a

C
1. The three main seasons of India are summer, winter and monsoon.
2. Tamil Nadu
3. The higher the altitude, colder is the place.

D
1. In India, the temperature continues to rise over the land in summer. The southwest monsoon winds, which originate from the Bay of Bengal

ANSWER KEY

cause rainfall in West Bengal, Assam and other northeastern states. Then these winds move westwards to the Indo-Gangetic Plains causing rainfall in this region. The plateau regions also receive rainfall during the monsoon. About 80 per cent of the total monsoon rainfall occurs from June to September. The rainfall in the desert region varies. Rajasthan and Ladakh receive minimum rainfall and Mawsynram in Meghalaya receives maximum rainfall. West Bengal receives some rainfall from thundershowers called kalbaishakhi from April to May. In southern India, the Coromandel region receives heavy rainfall during the winter months. The rainy season is a very important season as India is an agricultural country.

2. **Winters:** Winter in India lasts from December till February and till mid-March in some mountainous regions. January is the coldest month in India with temperatures dropping as low as 0 °C in the mountainous regions, 3 °C to 10 °C in northern regions, 20 °C to 25 °C in coastal regions. Tamil Nadu receives winter rainfall.

   Summers: Summer in India starts from the end of March. May and June are the hottest months in India. Temperature rises to almost 45 °C in the desert region. In the mountain regions, the average temperature stays between 23 °C to 25 °C.

   Monsoon: Monsoon season is from June to September. The rainfall varies in different places. Rajasthan and Ladakh receives the least rainfall and Mawsynram in Meghalaya receives the most rainfall in the world.

3. The tropical wet climate can be classified into tropical monsoon climate and tropical wet and dry climate. The Western Ghats, the Malabar Coast, southern Assam and the Andaman and Nicobar Islands experience tropical monsoon type of climate. The climate is characterized by moderate to high temperature and heavy rainfall. This kind of climate is found mainly in the peninsular region. Summers are extremely hot and the rainy season lasts from June till September. December is the coldest month.

E Refer to map Climatic Regions, page 88

Think Box

The equatorial region has some of the hottest places on the Earth. This happens because of the curvature of the Earth. The places located in this region receive the Sun's rays directly. Towards the magnetic poles of the Earth, the places receive slanting rays of the Sun and therefore, these places are not as hot.

Picture Study

1. Winter
2. From December to February

14. Natural Vegetation of India

Reflect

1. tidal forests
2. mountains and hills

Figure Out

When trees in a forest start burning, it is called a forest fire. A forest fire is caused when lightning strikes a dry tree, heat is generated in the undergrowth leading to a fire. It can also be caused by careless human activities.

DIY

1. Odisha
2. 5000
3. West Bengal

Workout

A 1. T 2. T 3. F 4. F

B 1. evergreen 2. mangrove or tidal 3. montane 4. monsoon type

C

1. The plants and trees that grow naturally in a region is called its natural vegetation.
2. The natural vegetation of India can be classified into six major types. These are:
   - Tropical evergreen forest
   - Dry deciduous forests
   - Tidal or mangrove forests
   - Deciduous or monsoon type forests
   - Semi-desert and desert vegetation
   - Mountain forests
3. Cactus, thorny bushes, date palms and grass grow in desert region.
4. Conservation of forests means not cutting down trees and saving our forests in its natural environment.

D

1. The natural vegetation of a region depends on several factors like the type of soil, latitude, altitude, amount of rainfall, climate and relief.
2. We should conserve forests because they:
   - prevent soil erosion.
   - purify the air and release oxygen through the process of photosynthesis.
   - cause rainfall.
   - provide shelter to birds and animals.
   - provide us with many valuable products.
   - add to the scenic beauty of a region.
   - prevent landslides in the hilly regions.

   It is the duty of all citizens to do their bit to preserve the natural environment. Cutting down trees, or deforestation, has an adverse effects on our planet, and it also causes damage to human and animal life.
3. The mountain vegetation varies according to altitude, rainfall and temperature. These forests are found in the Himalayan regions and in the

Nilgiri Hills. Trees such as teak, sal, bamboo, cover the higher regions, and coniferous trees such as pine, fir, rhododendrons, cedar, oak, and spruce are found near the foothills. Mangrove forests are found in swampy areas that are washed by sea water. They are found in the deltas of the rivers Ganga, Mahanadi, Godavari, Krishna and Kaveri.

4. Desert regions have thorny scrubs like babool, keekar, cactus, datepalm and grasses. Rainforests are found in regions that receive rainfall of above 200 cm annually.

E Map reference: India: Natural vegetation, page 93

Think Box

There is no vegetation as the ground is always covered with snow.

Picture Study

1. Mangrove
2. Tidal Forests
3. Such vegetation is found almost all along the eastern coast, especially in the large deltas formed by the rivers Ganga, Mahanadi, Godavari, Krishna and Kaveri. The most extensive rainforest are the Sundarbans, found in the Ganga-Brahmaputra delta region.

15. Agriculture

Reflect

1. wheat 2. cotton 3. rubber
4. millets 5. sugarcane 6. oilseeds

Figure Out

Jute is a natural fibre with golden and silky shine and hence called the golden fibre.

DIY

1. China 2. Arabica 3. China
4. America 5. India

Workout

A
1. agricultural
2. orchards
3. plantation
4. dairy, poultry

B 1. a 2. c 3. a 4. b

C

Crop	Climate Required	Soil	Regions
Rice	plenty of rainfall	loamy soil, clayey	West Bengal, Assam, Uttar Pradesh, Andhra Pradesh, Punjab, Tamil Nadu, Odisha, Bihar
Rubber	warm temperature, adequate rainfall	laterite soil	Slopes of eastern and Western Ghats, Kerala
Millet	high temperature, low rainfall	dry, sandy soil	Karnataka, Uttar Pradesh, Punjab, Kashmir, Bihar, Rajasthan, Gujarat
Tea	adequate rainfall	fertile soil rich in humus	Assam, West Bengal, Uttar Pradesh, Tamil Nadu, Kerala
Cotton	warm, moist climate, sunny dry days during ripening	black soil	Maharashtra, Gujarat, Karnataka, Andhra Pradesh, Punjab
Coconut	moist coastal climate, adequate rainfall	soil rich in salt, loamy soil	Kerala

D
1. Crops made for meeting food requirements of the country are called food crops.
2. Cash crops are grown by farmers to sell and earn money.
3. Sesame, mustard, castor, rapeseed, groundnut, linseed
4. Wheat, rice

E
1. Jute grows well in regions that receive heavy rainfall. A warm and humid climate is ideal for jute cultivation.
2. Wheat is a rabi or a winter crop. Cold winters and bright sunshine during ripening and harvesting are the ideal growing conditions for wheat. Uttar Pradesh is the leading producer of wheat in India, followed by Punjab. The states of Haryana and Madhya Pradesh, also produce a substantial amount of wheat.
3. Sugarcane grows well in regions with moderate rainfall and cool and dry weather. It grows best on well-drained alluvial soil.
4. Tea and coffee are beverage crops. Tea shrubs require fertile mountain soil rich in humus. Well-drained land with no stagnant water, which is mostly found on mountain slopes, is ideal for tea cultivation. Coffee grows best in a warm and moist climate with a spell of dry weather during the ripening period. Loamy and iron-rich soil is suitable for its growth. Coffee does not grow in frost, snowfall, high temperature above 30 °C and strong sunshine. It is generally grown under shady trees. Dry weather is necessary at the time of ripening of the berries.

F Map references: India: Rice producing regions, pg 99; India: Wheat producing regions, pg 100; India: Cotton and jute producing regions, pg 102

Think Box

Coconut grows best in moist coastal climate with adequate rainfall. Soil rich in salt and loamy soil of coastal regions and river valleys are ideal for its cultivation.

Picture Study

1. A tea plantation.
2. Require fertile, well drained soil rich in humus.
3. It grows well in warm to humid climate in the flatlands and hill slopes.

16. Industries

Figure Out

Raw materials are materials that are in their natural state, before they are processed or used in manufacturing. Finished product is the product that emerges at the end of a manufacturing process.

Workout

A 1. raw materials, people and capital
2. three   3. cottage
4. *plastic good, shell and lac products

B 1. T   2. T   3. T   4. T   5. F

C 1. Large scale, small scale, and cottage industries.
2. A small scale industry uses simple machines in small factories to produce finished goods.
3. A large scale industry employs a large number of skilled and well trained workers.
4. *Hand-embroidered saris, dress materials, block printing, handloom textiles, bamboo and cane craft, pottery, candles, handmade paper, locks and keys

D 1. Basic requirements to set up an industry are capital (money), raw materials, people and a good network of transport and distribution of finished products.
2. Large scale industries are very big factories and manufacturing units. They have a huge infrastructure and require a lot a capital. They employ a large number of skilled and well-trained workers. Large scale industries require a continuous supply of raw materials. Therefore, they are located in regions where raw materials are easily available. A large amount of fuel and electricity is required to run the units of a large scale industry. Large scale industries generally have a good distribution system to sell manufactured goods. They also have an efficient transport network for transporting finished products to different parts of the world. Modern technology is used for producing the goods in these industries. Some large scale industries in India are iron and steel, cement, petroleum, textile.
3. Small scale industry: A limited budget, simple machines used, low investment, few number of people employee, Distribution network to sell goods in a specified region Large scale industry: Big budgets, lot of raw materials required produced locally or transported from other places, a large amount of fuel and electricity is required to run the large machines, products sold in local and distant markets, employs a large number of skilled and well trained workers, they also have an efficient transport network for transporting finished products to different parts of the world.
4. Some of the harmful effects of industrialization are:
   - Chemical waste from the factories that flows into rivers and other water bodies affects the aquatic life.
   - Smoke released from the industries causes air pollution.
   - Solid waste from the industries is sometimes dumped on the land causing soil pollution.
   - Many industries use heavy machinery to produce goods. This causes noise pollution.

Think Box

Raw materials are available around the regions

Picture Study

1. Water pollution
2. Sewage, garbage and liquid wastes from households and industries
3. Sewage water should be treated in water plants before it is released.

17. Natural Resources

Reflect

Discussion on forests, animal life, land and natural resources. The natural heritage.

Figure Out

Geothermal energy is the heat energy generated and stored in the Earth.

Figure Out

A hybrid car runs on electric motor.

Workout

A 1. T   2. F   3. T   4. T

B 1. Plants, animals, fossils
2. Coal, oil, metals
3. Wind, water, sun
4. Sunlight

C 1. Natural resources are things obtained from nature.
2. Renewable and non-renewable
3. Inorganic natural resources come from abiotic sources such as water, soil, wind, minerals.
4. Coal, natural gas and petroleum are fossil fuels.

D 1. Renewable resources like wind, sunlight, animals are found in abundance in nature. They are constantly being replenished by natural processes. Whereas, non-renewable resources are those resources that exist in limited quantities.

Once consumed they cannot be replenished like petroleum, coal, minerals and metals.

2. The renewable resources of energy are wind, water, sunlight.
3. The threats to our natural resources are:
   - Overpopulation: The population of the world is increasing every day which in turn increases the consumption of natural resources.
   - Land use: There is an increase in the demand of agricultural land to meet the food requirements of an increasing population. As forests are being cut down for building cities, towns and roads there is less land left for growing crops.
   - Forests: Forest products such as wood and timber are being overused for constructing houses, offices and other buildings.
4. It is very important for us to use both renewable as well as non-renewable natural resources carefully. Since non-renewable resources take a long time to form, it is very important for us to preserve them. Therefore, people have developed ways where sunlight, water and wind are used in place of renewable sources to produce energy.

Think Box

*1. Electricity would be limited.
2. Petrol, diesel would not be available.
3. Industries using fossil fuel would shut down.

Picture Study

1. Coal
2. No, it is non-renewable
3. Air pollution
   Diseases caused by air pollution

18. Our Environment

Reflect

Living: Trees, dog, humans

Non-living: *aeroplanes, cars, buses, buildings, road

Figure Out

Answers will vary

Workout

A
1. two
2. Biotic
3. water, light, temperature, humidity, atmosphere, soil
4. globalization

B 1. b 2. c 3. d 4. a

C
1. Autotrophs and heterotrophs
2. Globalization is the process by which the world is becoming increasingly interconnected because of trade and cultural exchanges.
3. Interdependence is mutual dependence between two living things or between a living and non-living thing for survival.
4. Increased consumption leads to a depletion or reduction of natural resources and an increase in pollutants in the environment. Increased levels of carbon dioxide, methane and other harmful gases in our environment have caused global warming.

D
1. Autotrophs are producers like plants that make their own food. Heterotrophs are consumers. They depend on plants or animals for their food.
2. The abiotic component consists of all the non-living things and the physical environment. Some of the abiotic components of the environment are water, light, temperature, humidity, atmosphere and soil. Plants, humans and animals live on land. All plants grow on land. Land is also a source of minerals. All living things need water for their survival. Water is found on the Earth's in oceans, rivers, lakes, as underground water and as water vapour in the atmosphere. Our atmosphere is made up of different gases. Oxygen and carbon dioxide are the two most important gases that support life on the Earth. The ozone layer protects us from the harmful ultraviolet rays of the Sun.
3. Positive impacts of globalization are:
   a. A variety of products, sometimes at a cheaper price, are available.
   b. The employment opportunities and standard of living has improved because of globalization.
   c. Technological and medical developments from developed countries are available in the developing countries.
   d. Globalization has made people more aware of events occurring in different and faraway places of the world.

   Negative impacts of globalization are:
   a. Globalization can lead to unemployment as cheaper alternatives are available in other parts of the world.
   b. Globalization cause health-related issues. Diseases spread rapidly because of the movement of the people from one region to another. For example, bird flu and chikungunya.
4. Some of the negative effects of global warming are:

   The temperature on the Earth is rising gradually. The polar ice caps and glaciers are melting, leading to a rise in sea levels. It is believed that some inland regions face the danger of getting submerged because of the increase in the sea levels. Climate change causes extreme weather phenomena such as forest fires, droughts, violent storms and heavy unseasonal rainfall. Extreme changes in temperature can cause health problems. Global warming causes acid rain which damages crops and buildings. The depletion of the ozone layer harms plant and animal life on the Earth.

Think Box

All the well-educated and skilled people move to other countries to work. Our country loses their intelligentsia and expertise to make things better in our own country. It also means they improve the economy of other countries by giving their creative ideas.

Picture Study

1. Burning paper garbage
2. By educating people on the ill-effects of pollution and by segregating garbage for recycling.
3. It creates air pollution.

19. Natural Disasters

Reflect

*There is destruction of life, property and environment, there is disruption in the normal life of the people. Diseases will spread as a result. Government, NGOs, Relief organizations provide help to the affected people.

Figure Out

Mount Vesuvius

Workout

A 1. c 2. a 3. c 4. a 5. b

B 1. T 2. F 3. F 4. F 5. T

C 1. lava 2. earthquake 3. active 4. excess 5. epicenter

D
1. A natural disaster is a natural occurrence that has the potential to cause destruction to life, property and the environment.
2. An earthquake is a sudden shaking of the earth caused by movements deep inside the Earth.
3. A tsunami is a huge tidal wave. It can reach several kilometres inland and cause destructions.
4. Drought occurs when a region experiences long spells of no or less rainfall.

E
1. A volcanic eruption occurs when hot and molten rocks, ash and gases come out of the surface of the Earth through the openings of volcanoes. Sometimes volcanic eruptions also cause heavy rainfall. The hot magma that flows out from the volcano is called lava. The crack or opening through which the magma comes out is called a vent. The lava and ash coming out of a volcano keep piling up resulting in the formation of a mound.
2. Hurricane, typhoon and cyclone are different names given to very strong tropical storms caused by fast blowing rotating winds. These winds are known by different names in different countries. In India, they are called cyclones. In Japan, they are called typhoons and in America they are called hurricanes. Cyclones cause destruction and damage to life and property. Trees are uprooted, vehicles are upturned and buildings are damaged during cyclones.
3. *Safety rules during earthquakes
   - Do not run around in panic.
   - Do not sit near objects that can fall on you and hurt you.
   - If indoors, get under a table.
   - Do not use an elevator, use the stairs.
   - If outdoors, stand in an open area away from buildings and trees.

   Safety rules during tidal waves and tsunamis
   - Listen to warnings on the radio and television.
   - Avoid going near beaches.
   - Move to places located at an elevation.

   Safety rules during floods
   - Listen to flood warnings on the radio and television
   - Move to the roofs or upper storeys of the building, if evacuation is not possible.
   - evacuation is not possible.
   - Try to stock food, medicines and drinking water.
   - Contact the rescue team, friends or family for help.
4. Many agencies help us during natural disasters by providing immediate help and relief and later in rebuilding, and reconstructing roads and buildings. They provide medicines and food to the affected people. Some international agencies that are the United Nations and the Red Cross, and some national agencies are the army and air force, National Disaster Authority and the National Cadet Corps.

Think Box

Due to deforestation

Picture Study

A–floods, flooded street, excessive water

B–drought, parched, no rain

Test Yourself 1

A 1. a 2. a 3. b 4. b 5. b 6. b 7. b 8. b

B 1. homonids 2. copper 3. Bronze 4. Thomas Newcomen 5. Preamble 6. election

C
1. The discovery and the use of iron led to important developments in the history of humankind.

Agriculture: Iron was used for making sickles for harvesting crops and ploughshares for turning and digging the soil.

Trade: Trade relationships were established with distant regions. To carry out trade, money was needed. Hence, coins were made with iron. Money earned through trade was used to buy other useful things.

Occupation: People started taking up new occupations, such as construction, crafts and pottery. Nails and rivets were made by ironsmiths.

War: The use of iron also led to an increase in weapon production. Weapons such as swords, spears and arrowheads were made.There were constant fights amongst people and a powerful ruler was needed to bring in peace. Thus, the concept of kingship evolved.

Transport: During the Iron Age, vehicles, boats and ships were made by people. This improved the transport system and trade with distant lands grew.

2. Invention of the wheel was one of the most remarkable inventions of the Neolithic Age . This discovery brought about a change in the life of early humans, as they could now travel easily from one place to another, using carts fitted with wheels. They could also carry heavy loads on these carts. The potter's wheel was invented and used by humans during the next age. They used it for making pots to store grains.

3*. **Right to Equality:** The right to equality states that all people are equal before the law. People cannot be discriminated on grounds of religion, race, caste, gender or place of birth. Equality of opportunity in employment is also a part of the right to equality.

Right to Freedom: The right to freedom provides freedom of speech and expression to everyone. People have the freedom, to move throughout the country and to live in any part of India and to practise any occupation, profession or business. This right protects the life and freedom of all individuals.

Right to Freedom of Religion: This right gives people the right to choose and follow any religion they want.

Right Against Exploitation: The right against exploitation prohibits the employment of children below 14 years of age. No one is allowed to make someone work with little or no payment.

Cultural and Educational Rights: Cultural rights grant people the freedom to promote and nurture their culture. Educational rights ensure that all students have the right to get admission in any educational institute, irrespective of their caste, religion, race or language.

Right to Constitutional Remedies: The right to constitutional remedies empowers citizens to go to court, in case any of the fundamental rights are being denied to them or disregarded.

Right to Education: It entitles every child in the age group of 5 to 14 the right to free basic education.

4. i. The Rajya Sabha is also called the upper house. Members of the Rajya Sabha are not elected directly by the people. They are elected by the members of the legislative assemblies of all the states. The members of the Rajya Sabha are elected for a period of 6 years. One-third of its members retire every two years. The Rajya Sabha can have a maximum of 250 members.

   ii. Elections are an important process of the Indian democracy. Indians, above 18 years of age, have the right to elect leaders through a process called voting. They choose their leaders, who are answerable to the citizens. If the voters are unsatisfied with the performance of a leader, it is likely that they will not vote for them in the next election.

5. The legislature is also known as parliament or sansad in India. The legislature is the law-making body. The Indian Parliament has two houses—the Lok Sabha and the Rajya Sabha.

   The executive implements the laws passed by the legislature. The president, the vice president, the prime minister and the cabinet ministers, are all members of the executive. The president of India is the chief executive or the head of the country. He or she is elected for a period of 5 years by the members of the Lok Sabha, the Rajya Sabha and the state legislative assemblies.

   The Supreme Court is the highest court of law in India. The high courts and the district courts exist at the state and district level, respectively. The Supreme Court is headed by the chief justice of India. The main function of the judiciary is to settle disputes according to the laws and ensure that justice is delivered. It also ensures that the rights of all Indian citizens are protected

6. Factors affecting climate are:

   Latitude or distance from the equator. The places near the equator are hotter than the places located near the Poles.

   Altitude: The higher the elevation of a region, the colder it is.

   Distance from the sea: The places near the sea are neither too hot, nor too cold. However, the places located in the interiors of the continents are hot.

   Winds: Winds originating from the hills are cooler than the winds originating from the desert. Some winds carry moisture in them and cause rainfall.

Humidity: Places near the sea are very hot as the air has a lot of humidity.

7. The places near the equator are warmer than the places located near the Poles. Places near the equator receive the direct rays of the Sun. Places near the Poles receive the slanting rays of the Sun. As the rays have to travel for a longer distance, they lose their heat when they reach the poles whereas areas near equator retain heat from the Sun and Hence, we can say that the places near the equator are warmer than the places located near the Poles.

D
1. During the Paleolithic Age, early humans were hunter -gatherers and moved from place to place in search of food. They lived in caves and used tools made from stone, wood or bones. They began to communicate towards the end of this period.

   During Neolithic Age, early humans began to understand the importance of farming and moved towards a more settled life. Some important developments in this period were, invention of the wheel, domestication of animals, development in tools, pottery, concept of family and language for communication.
2. These days, people communicate using various means of communication. Telephones, letters and mobile phones are means of personal communication. Newspapers, television and radio are means of mass communication as they are used for communicating information to a large number of people at a time.
3. Every individual has some rights, regardless of who they are, where they live or what they do. These rights ensure that everyone is treated fairly. Some of the basic rights of all individuals are right to safety, right to freedom of speech, right to choose one's religion and right to food. A duty is a responsibility that people have towards their family, school, home, community or country. It is our duty to follow rules, save the environment and respect others
4. The weather is the condition of atmosphere over a short period of time. The climate is the average weather condition of a place over a long period of time. The weather may change in a few hours or daily. The climate does not change so frequently. Weather data is collected based on the reading at a specific time. Climate is described as the average temperature over a long period of time (generally 30 years).

E
1. Cleaning roads
2. Duty
3. Swachh Bharat Abhiyaan
4. Started by Government of India on 2 October, 2014.

F Diagram pg 64

Test Yourself 2

A 1. b 2. c 3. a 4. c 5. a

B 1. b 2. d 3. a 4. e 5. c

C
1. Richter's Scale
2. flood
3. raw material
4. hydroeclectricity
5. Sundarbans
6. Monsoon

D 1. T 2. F 3. T 4. F

E
1. An eclipse occurs when one celestial object comes in between us and another celestial object, blocking our view. Sometimes, while moving in their orbits, when the Moon and the Earth align with the Sun, then an eclipse occurs. Eclipses are of two kinds—solar and lunar. A solar eclipse occurs when the Moon passes in front of the Sun causing a shadow to fall on certain portions of the earth.
2. The Torrid Zone, The Temperate Zone and The Frigid Zone are the three temperature zones found in both the Northern and the Southern hemispheres. Diagram from pg 68
3. Monsoon is a period of heavy rains in summer in South Asia. The southwest monsoon winds, which originate from the Bay of Bengal bring rainfall to West Bengal, Assam and other northeastern states. Then, these winds move westward to the Indo-Gangetic Plains, causing rainfall in this region. The plateau regions also receive rainfall during monsoon. About 80 per cent of the total monsoon rainfall occurs from June to September. Rajasthan and Ladakh, the desert regions, receive minimum rainfall. Mawsynram in Meghalaya receives maximum rainfall. West Bengal receives some rainfall from thundershowers from April to May. In southern India, the Coromandel region receives heavy rainfall during the winter months. The monsoons or the rainy season is very important as India is an agricultural country.
4. The plants and trees that grow naturally in a region are called its natural vegetation. The natural vegetation of a region depends on several factors, like the type of soil, latitude, altitude, amount of rainfall, climate and relief.
5. Threats to Natural Resources are :
   i Overpopulation- The population of the world is increasing every day which in turn increases the consumption of natural resources.
   ii. Land overuse- There is an increase in the demand of agricultural land to meet the food requirements of an increasing population. Land is also required to construct the infrastructure of roads, offices, housing for a large population.
   iii. Deforestation- The cutting of trees and removal of forests increases soil erosion and air pollution. Forest products, such as wood and timber.

6. Globalization is the process by which the world is becoming increasingly interconnected because of trade and cultural exchanges. Improvements in transportation and communication, freedom of trade and easily available labour are some of the reasons that cause globalization Two merits are a variety of products, sometimes at a cheaper price, become available. The employment opportunities and the standard of living have improved due to globalization as more products become available in the markets*
7. We should stand in an open area during an earthquake to be away from buildings, wires, streetlights, bridges and other built places so that they may not fall on us while the earth is shaking. If indoors then drop down and take cover under a table.
8. Renewable Resources are natural resources such as air, water, sunlight, wind, forests, animals and soil. They can be replenished, that is, they do not get exhausted and are found in abundance on the Earth. Renewable resources are constantly being replenished by natural processes.

   Non-renewable resources are those resources that exist in limited quantities. They take hundreds of years to form. Once consumed, they cannot be replenished at the rate they are consumed. They are also known as exhaustible resources. Coal, petroleum, metals, minerals, oil and gas are non renewable resources.

F

1. The biotic component of the environment is made up of all living organisms, such as animals, plants, algae, fungi and bacteria. All living things live in an area or sphere of the Earth where life exists is called the biosphere. The abiotic component consists of all the non-living things and the physical environment. Some of the abiotic components of the environment are water, light, temperature, humidity, atmosphere and soil.
2. Large scale industries are very big factories and manufacturing units. They have a huge infrastructure and require a lot of capital. They employ a large number of skilled and well-trained workers. Large scale industries require a continuous supply of raw materials and an efficient transport network for transporting finished products to different parts of the world. Modern technology is used for producing the goods in these industries. Some large scale industries in India are iron and steel, cement, petroleum.

   Small scale industries involve a small group of people and run on limited budgets. They use simple machines to produce the goods. They also require a distribution network to sell their goods in specified regions. Shell and lac industry, plastic goods, agricultural tools, hosiery, toys and utensils are some small scale industries.
3. Food crops are grown to meet the food requirements of the country. Rice. wheat, cereals and pulses are food crops.

   Cash crops are grown by farmers to sell and earn money. Rubber, tea, coffee, jute, tobacco, sugarcane and cotton are cash crops.
4. In an eclipse, the umbra is the darkest part of the shadow of the Moon. It is the region where the Moon completely covers the Sun. The umbra becomes smaller as it reaches the Earth. The penumbra is the outer area of the shadow where the Moon is only covering a part of the Sun. The penumbra becomes bigger as it reaches the Earth.

G

1. It is a land slide.
2. No vehicular transport can ply on the route as the road is blocked. Food supplies to the region can be affected. It can also result in destruction and loss of life.*

H Map on pg 80

Worksheet Keys

Worksheet 1

A
1. hominids
2. mammals
3. hunter gatherers
4. fossils.

B
1. Early humans were called hominids.
2. The hunter gatherers ate fruits and roots of plants and also ate the flesh of animals that they hunted.
3. Hominids lived on the Earth for many years.
4. The remains of early humans were found in Africa.

C *Early humans lived in caves and treetops to protect themselves while modern men live in houses. Early men ate raw food and flesh of animals while modern men eat cooked food. They wore animal skin and used leaves to cover themselves while modern men wear dresses.

D We get information about early humans mainly from caves and rock shelters, tools and artefacts used by them, as well as fossils, bones and horns of animals. These are our sources of information.

Worksheet 2

A
1. d 2. a
3. b 4. c

B As early humans started growing food, they needed vessels to store them. Initially, baskets made of grass and thin branches of trees were used to store dry materials. However, to store cooked food, they needed different kind of vessels. They plastered the baskets with clay which, they discovered, hardened upon heating.

C Domestication of animals started during the Neolithic Age. Cows, goats, sheep, oxen and buffaloes were domesticated for meat and milk. Some animals were used for tilling soil in the field. Donkeys were used for transportation.

D Students would do themselves.

Worksheet 3

A
1. copper
2. west
3. Greek
4. Iron

B The discovery of iron was a turning point in the history of the world. Iron was strong and sturdy and ideal for making agricultural implements. Selling and buying of food grains started in towns and villages. Trade relationships were established with distant regions. To carry out trade, money was needed. Hence, coins were made with iron. Money earned through trade was used to buy other useful things. People started taking up new occupations such as construction, crafts and pottery. Nails and rivets were made by ironsmiths. An increase in the demand for cultivable land led to conflicts among people that ultimately caused wars. There were constant fights amongst people and a powerful ruler was needed to bring in peace. Thus, the concept of kingship evolved. During the Iron Age, vehicles, boats and ships were manufactured. This improved the transport system and trade with distant lands grew. Thus, Iron Age had a great impact on the life of the ancient people.

C As bronze was stronger than copper, early humans were able to make tools far better than those used in the past. An improvement in the quality of tools also improved farming techniques. This lead to an increased agricultural output and production of surplus grains. With enough grains in store, early humans started trade. The beginning of trade lead to the rise of cities.

D Using iron to make tools had many advantages. Iron was cheap and easily available. It was strong and sturdy, ideal for making agricultural implements. Iron was a better metal than bronze, as bronze had to be made by mixing copper and tin, which was not easily available. Iron could be easily extracted from its ore. Besides, bronze was softer than iron.

E Drawing and names will differ.

Worksheet 4

A
1. Thomas Newcomen
2. petroleum
3. Chinese
4. transmitters

B
1. Marco Polo travelled from Europe to Asia.
2. We can make video calls using a smart phone/laptop/computer.
3. Early humans used reed pens to write on clay tablets.

4. The first evidence of writing was found in Mesopotamia.

C 1. Mass communication is useful as it is used for communicating information to large a number of people at a time. Two means of mass communication are newspapers, television.

2. Modern methods of communication: Computers: We can use computers to send messages by electronic mail and the Internet to any part of the world. The Internet is a worldwide network, which is used to connect a computer to another computer in any part of the world. It helps in sending instant messages or pictures and is the most inexpensive mode of communication. We can also get useful and interesting information on any topic on websites.

   Satellite communication: Many man-made satellites are sent into the Earth's orbit. They pick up signals from the Earth and then send them back through transmitters. It is because of these satellites that we get to see what is happening in the other parts of the world instantly, or watch live telecasts of cricket and football matches sitting at home. Satellites also help meteorologists forecast weather or climate.

3. A great revolution in the field of transportation was the invention of the steam engine about 300 years ago. Thomas Newcomen was the first person who designed the steam engine, which was later improved by James Watt in 1781. The first train pulled by a steam engine was made about 200 years ago. Around the same time, ships running on steam engines were also used. Thus, travelling became easier and faster and heavy goods could be transported easily.

Worksheet 5

A 1. constitution

2. B. R. Ambedkar

3. central government

4. preamble

B 1. F 2. T 3. F 4. T

C 1. India is a vast country with 28 states and 8 Union Territories. To run such a big country, a system of government called parliamentary democracy has been adopted, which means, there is a central government for the entire country and state governments for each state. The central government looks after matters such as defence and foreign policy. The state government looks after the law and order and the internal issues of the states. The central and the state governments work together to ensure the well-being of the citizens of India.

2. All republics like India have a set of rules or principles that have to be followed by every citizen. These rules also help in governing the country. When India attained freedom, it was facing many socio-economic issues. Many people were uneducated and they were divided by the caste system. Equality among the people could be achieved only by making it a law so that everybody would get the same opportunities and benefits.

Worksheet 6

A 1. equality, respect, justice

2. Untouchability

3. right to education

4. monument

B 1. right

2. duty

3. right

4. right

5. duty

C 1. The fundamental duties for all the citizens of India: (any 3)

- To obey the laws in the Constitution and follow them
- To respect the National Flag and the National Anthem
- To protect the unity and honour of India
- To defend the country and offer our service when it is required
- To encourage peace and harmony among all the people of India and treat them like brothers and sisters
- To guard our environment and look after forests, rivers and wildlife
- To protect all public property such as monuments and historical sites

2. Cultural right grants the people the freedom to promote and nurture their culture. Educational right ensures that all students can get admission in any educational institute irrespective of their caste, religion, race or language. Right to Education entitles every child in the age group of 5 to 14 the right to free basic education.

3. Human rights are the basic freedoms that all humans have. These basic rights are based on principles of equality, respect and justice. Human rights are rights that allow us to live with dignity and help us avail our basic needs, such as food, shelter, and water.

Worksheet 14

A 1. f 2. d
3. a 4. b
5. c 6. e

B 1. tropical evergreen
2. rainfall, temperature, altitude
3. landslide
4. Van Mahotsav

C 1. The wood from trees found in the tidal forests is hard and they have aerial roots that that grow out of the stems.
2. The deciduous forests are found in regions that receive moderate to heavy rains.

   These forests are found in the lower slopes of the Himalayas, Assam, West Bengal, Bihar, Jharkhand, Chhattisgarh, Odisha, Karnataka, Maharashtra and some parts of the Sutlej-Ganga Plain.
3. We should conserve forests because:
   - they prevent soil erosion.
   - they clean the air and release oxygen during
   - photosynthesis.
   - they cause rainfall.
   - they provide shelter to birds and animals.
   - they provide us with many valuable products.
   - they add to the scenic beauty of a region.
   - they prevent landslides in the hilly regions.
4. There is no vegetation in the highest regions as it is snow capped all around the year. The snow never melts for any vegetation to grow.
5. Social Forestry is the management and protection of forests and planting of new forests on barren and deforested land for helping environmental, social and rural development.

Worksheet 15

A 1. coffee
2. Biogas
3. coconut
4. orchard
5. sugarcane

B 1. kharif
2. rabi
3. rabi
4. kharif
5. kharif

C 1. Orchards are fruit farms. A variety of fruits are grown in the orchards. Mangoes, apples, cherries, lychees, oranges, sweet lime, pineapples are grown in different parts of India. Melons and watermelons are grown along the rivers where the soil is sandy.
2. Livestock or animal rearing contributes significantly in the development of the Indian economy. Dairy, poultry and fish are some of the important sectors of livestock rearing in India. India has one of the world's largest livestock resources.
3. Millets are grown in the drier areas in both the summer and winter seasons. It can withstand drought and heavy rainfall.
4. The Green Revolution in India began in the 1960s when the government of India introduced schemes and measures to improve the agricultural productivity in the country. The farmers were provided high yielding variety of seeds (HYV). This, along with use of fertilizers, more irrigation and improved methods of farming, increased the crop yields, especially of wheat and rice. The increased production not only brought more income for the farmers but also helped to make India self-sufficient in food grains.

Worksheet 16

A 1. b 2. b
3. a 4. a

B 1. manufacturing units
2. coal/diesel/petrol/natural gas
3. transportation network
4. technology
5. pollution
6. industrial development

C 1. Industrialization is the setting up of industries to manufacture goods and machinery required by the people of a country. Goods are produced for consumption within the country and for exports.
2. Industrial development is very important for the economy of a country as industries provide jobs and employment to people, which in turn increases their income.
3. Cottage industries often receive help from the government and some non-governmental organizations for design, quality control and sale and distribution of products. The money made from the sale is given to the family running the industry. Exhibitions and fairs are organized to promote the sale of goods.

4. Large scale industries require a continuous supply of raw materials. Therefore, they are located in regions where raw materials are easily available.

Worksheet 17

A
1. Fossil fuels like coal, petroleum and natural gas are found very deep down in the earth. They are formed over thousands of years from the buried remains of plants and animals.
2. Natural resources such as air, water, sunlight, wind, forests, animals and soil are renewable resources.

B
1. salt, tidal energy
2. 3%
3. Biotic
4. solar panels, electricity
5. Tamil Nadu, West Bengal
6. refinery

C
1. Soil is an important natural resource as plants and trees grow in it. Soil is one of the main factors which decides the type of crops, farming and agriculture practices of any region.
2. CNG is a cleaner fuel as it does not give out fumes that pollute the air when used to run vehicles.
3. There is an increase in the demand of agricultural land to meet the food requirements of an increasing population. Land is also required to construct the infrastructure of roads, offices, housing for a large population. Forests are cut down to accommodate the growing needs population putting a tremendous pressure on land use and also overcrowding.

Worksheet 18

A

1. e 2. c

3. d 4. b

5. a

B
1. The population of the world has increased phenomenally and so have our needs. Increased consumption leads to a depletion or reduction of natural resources and an increase in pollutants of the environment. Increased levels of carbon dioxide, methane and other harmful gases in our environment have caused global warming. This happens when the pollutants do not allow the heat to escape from atmosphere, making the Earth hotter.
2. The effects of global warming are:
   - The temperature on the Earth is rising gradually. The polar ice caps and glaciers are melting leading to a rise in sea levels. It is believed that some inland regions face the danger of getting submerged because of increase in the sea levels.
   - Climate change causes extreme weather phenomena such as, droughts, violent storms and heavy unseasonal rainfall.
   - Extreme changes in temperature can cause health problems.
   - Global warming causes acid rain which damages crops and buildings.
   - The depletion of the ozone layer harms plants and animal life on the Earth.
3. The biosphere has two types of living things – producers or autotrophs, and consumers or heterotrophs. Autotrophs make their own food whereas, heterotrophs depend on plants and animals for their food. Human beings and animals are heterotrophs as we depend on plants for our food. Plants are producers and we are consumers.
4. Every form of life on the Earth is dependent on other living things. Living things also depend on natural resources such as air, soil and water. A change in one of the components affect the other component of the environment. For example, a growth in the population of a particular species affects the environment. In turn, these environmental factors are affected by the size and growth rate of the population.

Worksheet 19

A

1. h 2. g

3. b 4. c

5. d 6. a

7. f 8. e

B The study of earthquakes is called seismology. Scientists who study earthquakes are called seismologists. Seismologists try to predict earthquakes so that people can move to safer areas before an earthquake strikes. The instrument used to measure the intensity and duration of an earthquake is called a seismograph or seismometer. Earthquakes are measured with a Richter Scale. The Richter Scale measures earthquakes with intensities ranging from 1 to 10.

C Forest fires can occur because of lightning or due to the heat generated by rotting plant or animal matter. Sometimes, forest fires are also caused by the release of hot lava from volcanoes or because of the carelessness of human beings.

D A natural disaster is a natural occurrence that has a potential to cause great destruction of life, property and the environment. It may lead to loss of life of humans and animals, spread of diseases, disruption of transport and communication, shortage of food, evacuation to safer places.

E Droughts are long periods of very low rainfall. They make the land parched and dry, as a result of which the soil cracks. Droughts cause great distress to the farmers as their crops die. Long periods of drought lead to famine and acute shortage of food and water. Large number of human and animal lives are lost during a famine.